Multiple Intelligences and Portfolios

A Window into the Learner's Mind

Evangeline Harris Stefanakis

Introduction by Bruce Torff
Forewords by Deborah Meier
and Thomas Hehir

with contributions from
Lynn F. Stuart, Jill Harrison Berg,
and Kathleen Guinee

HEINEMANN
Portsmouth, NH

Heinemann
A division of Reed Elsevier Inc.
361 Hanover Street
Portsmouth, NH 03801–3912
www.heinemann.com

Offices and agents throughout the world

Library of Congress Cataloging-in-Publication Data
Stefanakis, Evangeline Harris.
  Multiple intelligences and portfolios : a window into the learner's mind /
Evangeline Harris Stefanakis
    p. cm.
  Includes bibliographical references and index.
  ISBN 0-325-00363-7 (alk. paper)
  1. Learning, Psychology of. 2. Multiple intelligences. 3. Portfolios in
education. I. Title.

LB1060 .S82 2002
370.15'23—dc21

                                                          2001051629

Editor: Danny Miller
Production: Elizabeth Valway
Cover design: Jenny Jensen Greenleaf
Director of technology: Jeff Northrop
CD-ROM development: Harbour Light Productions
Cover and CD-ROM photographs by Kathleen Guinee
Typesetter: Argosy
Manufacturing: Steve Bernier

Printed in the United States of America on acid-free paper
06 05 04 03 02 VP 1 2 3 4 5

This book is dedicated to my daily teachers—
To my mother, Irini, the first one who sat beside me as a learner,
To my husband, Manny, an artist and adventurer,
To Rianna, my daughter, a spirit of curiosity and exploration,
To Nikias, my son, an athlete and scholar always asking hard questions,
To Alexandros, a naturalist and budding musician, a joyous spirit, and
finally to the multiple intelligences of each individual
which I sincerely hope will be better understood.

Contents

To supplement this chapter, a collection of tools for teachers to use to develop a MI student profile are offered as PDF files on the CD.

The CD shows how a single portfolio can help illustrate the profile of a learner and help teachers gather data for a student's MI profile.

This part of the CD introduces Bela Bhasin's classroom portfolio system. It shows the difference between grade 1 and grade 2 portfolios. Portfolios of three children from Bela's class illustrate individual differences and individual children's distinct profiles.

In this chapter, Lynn F. Stuart of the Cambridgeport School provides an overview of assessment as documentation and celebration that is embodied in her school community. Her schema of a comprehensive assessment system which includes portfolios, student records, teachers' records, Massachusetts standards-based assessments, and standardized testing is explained as the context for the teachers' work that follows. Graduation by portfolio is introduced along with celebrations for the community.

The CD shows student work samples from the Learning in Revolutionary Projects. Grades 5 and 6 demonstrate their focus on historic learning by sharing their work during a Portfolio Celebration Day. Examples from three students (grades 5/6) are presented to illustrate the developmental perspective of older elementary students as they reflect on their work and learning, show the great variation among students, and illustrate learning challenges in both boys and girls. The teacher resources to create MI Thematic Curriculum Projects and Portfolio Resources are included as PDF files. Sample unit assignment sheets are also included to show how Sarah Fiarman moved from planning to implementation.

On the CD, Jill Harrison Berg's format for using traveling portfolios with adolescents is presented. Her examples feature the work of a single subject portfolio in the humanities area. The design and use of portfolios for home-school dialogue is featured in this chapter and on the CD as a model for middle school practitioners. Sample reflection tools, work tags, rubrics for graduation, and portfolio cover letters are also included.

Foreword by Deborah Meier

Rediscovering an "old" idea in a new light is always particularly exciting. Evangeline's essential book, *Multiple Intelligences and Portfolios* reverberates with the ideas that led us nearly twenty years ago to "invent" a system of portfolio review for graduate students from Central Park East Secondary Schools. At the time, our ideas weren't connected to the idea of multiple intelligences—or at least not consciously. We were seeking a way to focus our work as *teachers* and the work of our students on something more authentic than standardized test scores and/or students having simply completed a set of mandated course titles. We were, in Ted Sizer's terms, seeking standards for student work. To do this meant that, as adults, we'd have to ask ourselves what intellectual habits and understandings mattered most to us, and then think about how young people could "show us" they had achieved them—and what an "acceptable" level of such achievement might look like. Neither of these tasks was commonplace in the high schools we knew best. I think we, *as a faculty*, also liked the idea because it fostered democratic habits in a way that traditional assessment didn't [the capacity to respond to real audiences, and take responsibility for and thus defend one's work and ideas]. The whole process required the exercise of multiple judgments by the student but also—and this was important to us—by the review committee of *adults*. It was a model of respect for such human judgments, and in ways that insisted that the object of the exercise—the *individual* student—remained an *active participant* in all such judgments. We liked the democratic implications of this process. Over the years I have grown to see many more reasons why this approach works, *and* carries with it such power and energy.

Evangeline is right: it also corresponds well to what we know about the human mind itself.

We always "knew" that portfolios tapped into individual interests and styles, but that was not at the time our central argument. As I read this wonderful book, that captures the essence of portfolio work, this dimension became more and more interesting and important. After all, the studies of our graduates always noted that one of the reasons alumni gave for what the Central Park East schools did for them were nurture their passions, provide support for their individual interests, and treat their idiosyncrasies *with respect*. It was clearer and clearer to me that the kids we *most* ought to worry about were those who had no strong interests, no focus, no passion, no particular style! When I look back on my own children's lives, I recall with what pleasure I greeted my son's announcement that he was devoting himself to freestyle Frisbee. It wasn't my first (or second) interest of choice, but what it signaled was my son's capacity to take on something for himself, not just to please others or for some external utilitarian gain—valuable as these may also be.

It turns out my instinct was right—and much of the work of Gardner that Evangeline outlines here, more like the rather different but complementary work of Pat Carini and The Prospect Center, helps us see why this intuition was accurate.

Behind portfolio assessments is a respect for our human variability, our capacity to tackle common concerns in special ways. Behind portfolio assessments, as they become more than just a final way to make judgments, is *authentic work* that is an integral part of the culture of a school. The coming together of a community around "what matters"—around agreed-upon commonalities—need not, this book reminds us, lead to standardized "common" testing and standardized schooling. Rather, such sharing of "what matters" can be the impetus for celebrating respect for differences as well.

Of course, the delight of this book also lies—perhaps above all—in the myriad, real-life examples, the showing of how portfolios work in practice for individual children and schools. Evangeline's intimate knowledge and respect for what goes on in real schools is something I know firsthand; *and* it comes through also in this book. We in the field are enormously indebted to her for putting this work together, and for imbedding the sometimes misused and abused slogan of performance assessment into a richer and deeper context as well as in living experiences and examples.

—Deborah Meier
Coalition of Essential Schools–Boston
Mission Hill School
Boston, Massachusetts

Foreword by Thomas Hehir

As a practitioner, Evangeline Stefanakis faced a situation common to many special educators: teaching children whose abilities and potential were poorly reflected in commonly used assessment instruments. Parents of children with disabilities as well as many teachers have known that testing instruments that focus heavily on either linguistic or mathematic domains often miss many of the strengths children bring to learning situations and ultimately to life. Worse yet, the narrow focus of many educational programs on "remediating" deficiencies in these commonly assessed domains has greatly limited the educational experience of countless disabled children. As educational programs focus on the weaknesses, not the strengths, of children, is it any wonder that children with disabilities drop out of school at twice the rate of nondisabled children and suffer high levels of unemployment and underemployment? In my view, the degree to which narrow assessment practices have driven inappropriate educational programming is significant.

As a special educator who taught in a vocational high school, I found the logic of the lens of multiple intelligences reinforced by many of my former students. I saw students who had struggled mightily with reading and writing and who excelled in shop classes. I recall a student with mental retardation who survived a major layoff at his company because he was a superior machine operator with terrific interpersonal skills. I had students who went on to successful careers who would have likely dropped out of high school if their "intelligences" in other areas were not nurtured. Research in special education increasingly provides support for my own anecdotal experience as well as the theory of multiple intelligences. In a comprehensive study of eight thousand high school students with disabilities, Wagnor found that concentrating in vocational classes at the high school level was associated with superior results in employment, income, and community integration.

This book and the theories that undergird it address a critical issue of practice: assessing the whole child for the purpose of developing more enriched educational opportunities. As such, this book seeks to address a persistent problem in special education practice. Too often assessment has been used primarily to sort and label children, not as a vehicle for improving practice. How many teachers have complained that the tests typically administered to a child as part of the Individualized Education Plan (IEP) process are irrelevant to their practice? Clearly, the approach developed by Dr. Stefanakis, utilizing Howard Gardner's theory of multiple intelligences, is a major step forward. This approach is child-focused and classroom-based and holds great potential for expanding educational opportunity.

Stefanakis' work takes on even greater importance in the context of contemporary special education policy, embodied in the 1997 amendments to the Individuals with Disabilities Education Act (IDEA 97). One goal of these amendments is to eliminate the practice of moving students into inferior educational environments dominated by low expectations. A specific requirement of law states IEP teams must address how the student will access the general education curriculum. Further, students must now be included in accountability systems with appropriate accommodations and modifications. The comprehensive approach to assessment contained in this book provides a foundation upon which an accessible educational house can be built.

I would be remiss if I were to imply that this book is relevant only to special education practice. One thing we have learned over and over again is that practices that have proven to be effective with students with disabilities are usually beneficial for other students as well. Students with disabilities are not the only children who benefit from carefully tailored personalized instruction. Theories of multiple intelligences as well as the practices advocated in this book can enrich the education of all children.

Finally, I would like to end by expressing my admiration for my colleague Van Stefanakis. She has taken on a long-standing problem in practice—the inappropriate assessment of children's ability—and tied a promising theory to improved modes of practice. She has implemented her new ideas in real schools in a manner that is deeply respectful of teachers and students. The product of her work is therefore both visionary and practical. As such, she has made a great and unfortunately rare contribution to improving practice.

—Thomas Hehir
Harvard Graduate School of Education
Cambridge, Massachusetts

Acknowledgments

So many great minds and spirits have helped this book come to life that I can only thank the recent characters in the story!

This work is deeply indebted to the work of Howard Gardner, whose theory of multiple intelligences helped me, as a special educator and school psychologist, understand and explain the capabilities in so many children who have failed in schools in the United States and abroad. Many students I assessed, who were labeled learning disabled, had exceptional talents in the arts, music, or in other domains. This plagued me as a diagnostician. Gardner's groundbreaking theory offered the language and ideas to recognize the unique profiles of individuals who were more than just *word* smart. As a colleague at Project Zero, Howard helped me deepen my thinking about learning and teaching. His theory and invitation to explore its ramifications in practice has encouraged me to work to see that all children can learn, if we teach them.

To Danny Miller, the second most vital person in this manuscript's journey. As my editor at Heinemann, he steadfastly encouraged me to write this book, and to capture children's work on a CD-ROM. His vision of a multiple intelligences (MI) approach to the book and its CD, along with his excellent feedback and his advocacy, was the true catalyst for the manuscript and its eventual completion.

To my Project Zero (PZ) colleagues who taught me about MI theory and portfolios during our work with the Massachusetts Schools Network. To Joe Walters and Steve Seidel, the portfolio pioneers, whose rich conversation about student work is mirrored in the text and on these pages. They remain the dynamic duo who brought me to PZ and drove with me across Massachusetts, school to school, for three years actively

building portfolio cultures. My deep commitment to collaborative assessment comes from sitting beside Steve Seidel, the
developer of these protocols. I am grateful for this learning
opportunity and pleased to join him now as a faculty colleague.

To my colleagues in assessment—to Vito Perrone, my advi-
sor on research in teacher's classroom assessment over the past
ten years; to Dennie Wolf, my first portfolio teacher; and to
Eleanor Duckworth, who insisted that I look carefully and
observe children and their work. I cannot thank each of you
enough for your inspiration, advice, and wonderful ideas. To
Brenda Engel, a colleague and friend from my Lesley College
years, another pioneer in portfolio assessment whose writing
grounded me in the wonder of how individuals learn. Brenda's
mentorship over fifteen years has influenced me deeply, more
than she can imagine.

To the practitioners whose talents I believe are often not recognized and appreciated in professional educational circles. To
Lynn F. Stuart, whose visionary leadership in teaching, learning, and assessment has helped create a phenomenal learning
community at the Cambridgeport (CPort) School. Over our
fifteen years as colleagues, I have learned so much from her and
her teachers about how a community of learners can become a
collaborative culture. Although I know this book was more
than she bargained for, her continued support in talking and
writing, through multiple drafts, strengthens almost every
page.

To Bela Bhasin, Sarah Fiarman, and Jill Harrison Berg,
who found the time to let me sit beside them to document
their wisdom about portfolio assessment. I am proud to have
been able to capture their talents as educators and colleagues
in multifaceted ways—in words, in children's work, and in
pictures. They met me after school, sat for interviews, read
drafts, shared portfolios, helped get permissions, and did all
one could hope for in making their work visible. Their commitment to teaching teachers about portfolio work is truly
amazing and I can only marvel at what I have learned!

To other Cport faculty—Zevey Steinetz, Nili Perlmutter, Frederick Won Parks, Sylvia Soderberg, Laurie Cleveland, and Kelly Tarmey, whose thoughts and materials about portfolios are reflected in these pages as well. Many other administrators and teachers at the Cambridgeport School and in the district contributed to experimentation with portfolios and shared their craft for this work: Meynardo Gutierrez, Claire Lundberg, Kathy MacDonald, Liz Fuchs, Lenora Jennings, and Maryann MacDonald. Each one of them, as educators, as leaders, and as learners continue to collect, select, and reflect on student work to try to understand the multiple intelligences of Cambridge children.

To colleagues at the Education Publishing Group who provided so much in helping these manuscripts evolve from an idea into print. To Karen Mahoney, who introduced me to Heinemann and encouraged me throughout the writing process—from prospectus to finality—my gratitude to her as a colleague and writer is immense. To Doty Riggs, my faithful editor, now friend, who keeps me on track as I patiently rework my language and usage so that the ideas get clearer on the page.

To my research assistant and doctoral student, Kathleen Guinee, who spent nine months taking photos, recording interviews, visiting classes, doing observations, and helping to compile the CD materials. Her technological skills are the heart and soul of the CD's rich content. She organized the data, created storyboards, and celebrated the wonder of these children and the teachers at the Cambridgeport School. To other students from my Understanding Learning Challenges course who see the connection between MI theory and students who learn differently. Special thanks to Amy Lakin, a gifted special educator, who contributed editorial help. To Karen Pelletier, who helped scan children's portfolios as she deepened her leadership skills in curriculum and assessment.

To Linda Greyser and to Tony Wagner, colleagues from HGSE and collaborators on our Athens College Project in

Greece. They taught me to frame new questions about teachers' portfolios. Together they took portfolios to Greece and asked questions and offered feedback on the power of portfolios as a vehicle to keep teachers learning. Many of the graphics created in the book were drafted on plane rides with them. To the teachers of Athens College who found ways to make portfolios learning tools for their communities. Articulating MI and portfolios in English and in Greek deepened my commitment to write about it all someday.

There is really one person I must remember who is not here—my father—he would be proud that I captured the art and the words of diverse learners who face language and learning challenges as he did in school. He knew, I believe, that challenging children needed my attention. Perhaps their talents will be understood!

Introduction

On Intelligence and Assessment

It is easy to imagine why Howard Gardner's theory of multiple intelligences (Gardner 1983, 1993) has risen to prominence on the educational scene in the United States and abroad. To begin with, "MI" is a clear and straightforward theory that can be summarized in short order—people have at least eight different specialized intelligences, not a single all-purpose one. Moreover, MI appeals to advocates of child-centered education; in Gardner's hopeful framework, all students have areas of relative strength. MI also works to counter our educational system's increasing reliance on standardized tests, providing the welcome argument that there is more to the child than what the test scores show. Finally, MI appeals to educators focused on diversity issues, concerning language, culture, ethnicity, gender, and other issues. MI is agreeable to educators who seek quality education and social justice for all learners, across the diversity that comprises our society.

As a result, Gardner's theory remains very popular. Many university education schools teach MI in courses in human development and general methods. Professional development events centered on MI are so commonplace that there's hardly a teacher left in America who is unfamiliar with MI. There are MI books, articles, and videos in extraordinary abundance, such that some catalogs feature a discrete section on MI alongside such typical categories as literacy and science education. Clearly, MI ranks among the most significant developments on the educational scene in the last half century.

MI and Curriculum Development

MI theory calls for diversification of educational practices to encompass the multiple intelligences, in terms of *curriculum and instruction* (planning and delivery of units and lessons) as well as *assessment* (evaluation of learning outcomes) (Gardner, Torff, & Hatch 1996). But the MI world has been especially focused in the area of curriculum development.

Many schools in the United States have gone all out, remaking themselves as "MI schools" by placing the theory at the center of school-wide curriculum-development initiatives. The Key School in Indianapolis was the first, and remains among the best known (Kornhaber & Krechevsky 1994), and it has been followed by many others. For instance, the staff at Wyandot Elementary School in Dublin, Ohio raised grant money to implement a schoolwide educational reform plan that focused on using MI to motivate new and more diversified learning experiences for children. The teachers developed curriculum pressing the eight intelligences into use as skills to be strengthened (MI as curriculum), and also as vehicles for learning content (MI in curriculum). More visibly, an MI-based initiative at the New City School in St. Louis resulted in a book that chronicles what goes on when a school employs MI to write new curriculum (Hoerr 2000). Further evidence that MI has been chiefly a curriculum-development tool appears in the MI literature, which focuses on creating MI-inspired activities in schools (e.g., Fogarty 1995; Lazear 1999).

MI and Assessment

MI has been less developed in relation to assessment (Torff & Warburton in press). MI and assessment was the theme of an exploratory volume edited by Torff (1996) featuring several views on how MI relates to performance assessments, portfolios, rubrics, and other alternative assessment procedures. These explorations broke new ground, but the book's authors concluded that much work was needed in developing MI-compatible assessments. The promise of MI-in-assessment remained largely unfulfilled until Evangeline Harris Stefanakis wrote the book you are now reading.

The longtime dearth of MI assessment work is ironic, given that MI was formulated in part as a critique of contemporary assessment procedures (Torff & Gardner 1999). Gardner, reacting to the increasing influence of standardized tests, advanced MI theory as a departure from "psychometrics as usual"—the practice of giving students multiple-choice tests for the making of important educational decisions (e.g., college admissions). Such tests filter the individual's various intelligences through the logical-mathematical and linguistic intelligences—the ones involved in the testing procedure. As a result, typical testing procedures provide a distorted view of all the intelligences and grossly underemphasize the visual-spatial, musical, bodily-kinesthetic, naturalistic, intrapersonal, and interpersonal intelligences.

In this book, Stefanakis supports Gardner's view that the intelligences ought to be assessed in ways that are *intelligence-fair*—that allow the functioning of the intelligences to be assessed without being measured by proxy through other intelligences. Intelligence-fair assessment has two key components.

The first is the need for contextualized assessment, which means that students do the same things in the assessment tasks as they regularly do in the classroom. Contextualized assessments should be real-world performances and not artificial concoctions. Long ago it was observed that animals in zoos act differently than they do in the wild, causing zoologists to conclude that animal behavior depends on its context. It follows that a standardized-testing environment might be just as alien and artificial for test takers, altering their behavior and undermining the validity of the test. This issue is often called "ecological validity"—the extent to which the means of assessment correspond to the way the person works in the real world (Cole, Hood, & McDermott 1978). According to MI theory, human performances must be examined in context if assessment procedures are to be valid.

The second component of intelligence-fair assessment is the need for assessments that are ongoing—that is, structured with repeated data collection events, unlike one-shot-deal psychometric tests. A photograph hints at the action going on; a series of photographs tell more of the story of the scene's action; a movie provides even more detailed information. Ongoing assessments allow the development of the person's knowledge and skill to be charted—as in collections of student work documented in portfolios.

A true assessment can be made only by evaluating a child's performances over time, using multiple measures. Intelligence-fair assessments are not easy to design (although Stefanakis' book capably shows the reader how educators have learned to do this with portfolios). Intelligence-fair assessments are often lengthy, difficult, and costly, whereas psychometric tests are quick, easy to score more reliably, and inexpensive.

Then there's the problem of the inferential character of the intelligences. According to Gardner, educators can only infer how the intelligences are operating from an individual's work (Gardner 1983, 1993, 1999). It is impossible to "measure" the intelligences directly, or even "see" them. The operations of intelligences in isolation are visible only in rare cases of savants or prodigies. For most people, the intelligences operate in combination, with several intelligences supporting virtually all human thought and action. The student's work speaks only to these combinations and not to the function of individual intelligences, and an analysis of individual intelligences will certainly be misleading. Moreover, the function of the intelligences is influenced by contextual factors. One never sees, for example, linguistic intelligence *per se;* one instead sees linguistic intelligence in a particular context of use. Not all accomplished poets are good journalists, or vice versa, but both use linguistic intelligence in vastly different contexts. There is no such thing as context-free assessment, and a set of eight independent tests constitutes an unacceptably artificial context.

A student's work provides a brief glimpse of his/her intelligences, but never a direct window on them, no matter how hard educators look. In this book, Stefanakis echoes Gardner's call for assessments that focus not on measuring individual intelligences (e.g., linguistic intelligence), but on evaluating valued performances as evidenced in students' work (e.g., ability to write a clear topic sentence for a paragraph).

Taking stock, MI is remarkably popular as a way to view the human mind, and it has been implemented extensively in curriculum development. The need persists to develop assessment procedures that are congruent with the theory, given the importance Gardner places on alternative assessments. Because of the complex theoretical status of the intelligences, assessments that are true to MI's vision have proven difficult to design and interpret.

MI and Portfolio Assessment

Here is a book that moves courageously into the breech. Stefanakis uses portfolio assessment as a way to assess children's work across the full range of valued intelligences, without going a bridge too far—that is, without trying to "read" the child's individual intelligences by looking at his/her work. Refraining from assigning numerical scores (or even commenting extensively) on isolated intelligences, the book shows what intelligence-fair assessment looks like. It focuses on MI as a way to motivate a welcome diversification of curriculum and instruction, while concentrating in the assessment process on valued real-world skills.

Multiple Intelligences and Portfolios: A Window into the Learner's Mind provides a practical and classroom-based approach to implementing portfolio assessment. As such, the book helps teachers to *collect* portfolio data, encourage students to *select* pieces for inclusion in a portfolio, and *reflect* on the work and the processes by which it was made (and also to generate strategies for improvement). Stefanakis has written a useful primer on portfolio assessment that is prescriptive and clear for newcomers to this approach—and yet substantive and detailed for experienced portfolio mavens.

Stefanakis also shows how MI and portfolios *personalize* learning. The relationships and roles of teachers and students change when these assessment alternatives are implemented. Traditional psychometric assessments ask children to repeat what adults think they should know—and never ask students to evaluate their own work. This removes the student from the assessment process, except to wait for the scores to be delivered. Such an arrangement puts teachers and administrators in the role of evaluator—the select group empowered to decide how the student is doing.

This book explores the results when all that is turned upside down, when students and teachers collaborate to evaluate student work and decide what's next. Most notably, there is a fundamental change in power relationships in the classroom. Portfolios allow the teacher to "sit beside" learners rather than "stand over" them—a power sharing arrangement. By allowing students to participate in their own assessment, a more favorable classroom climate is created, with great benefit to the personal/emotional development of children, not to mention their academic progress. Not only does this book show how restructuring assessment can better capture what students can do, it shows how focusing on individual learners yields all sorts of benefits for the community.

Multiple Intelligences and Portfolios ably delivers on the promise inherent in MI theory's call for intelligence-fair assessment. Stefanakis describes assessments that capture all of children's abilities, not just the ones easily captured on tests. And she makes compelling the case that such assessments transform the classroom into a more nutritious place for each individual child.

Bruce Torff
Hofstra University

References

Cole, M., Hood, M., and McDermott, R. 1978. "Concepts of Ecological Validity." *The Quarterly Newsletter of Institute for Comparative Human Development, 2*, 34–37.

Fogarty, R. 1995. *Integrating Curricula with Multiple Intelligences: Teams, Themes, and Threads*. Palatine, Il: IRI Skylight.

Gardner, H. 1983, 1993. *Frames of Mind: The Theory of Multiple Intelligences*. New York: Basic Books.

——— 1993. *Multiple Intelligences: The Theory in Practice*. New York: Basic Books.

——— 2000. *Intelligence Reframed: Multiple Intelligences for the 21st Century*. New York: Basic Books.

Gardner, H., Torff, B., and Hatch, T. 1996. "The Age of Innocence Reconsidered: Preserving the Best of the Progressive Tradition in Psychology and Education." In D. Olson and N. Torrance (Eds.), *Handbook of Psychology in Education: New Models of Learning, Thinking, and Teaching*. Cambridge, MA: Basil Blackwell.

Hoerr, T. 2000. *Becoming a Multiple Intelligences School*. Alexandria, VA: Association for Supervision and Curriculum Development.

Kornhaber, M., and Krechevsky, M. 1994. "Expanding Definitions of Teaching and Learning: Notes from the MI Underground." In P. Cookson, (Ed.) *Creating School Policy: Trends, Dilemmas, and Prospects*. New York: Garland Press.

Lazear, D. 1999. *Eight Ways of Knowing: Teaching for Multiple Intelligences*. Palatine, Il: IRI Skylight.

Torff, B. (Ed.) 1996. *Multiple Intelligences and Assessment*. Palatine, Il: IRI Skylight.

Torff, B. & Gardner, H. 1999. "The Vertical Mind: The Case for Multiple Intelligences." In M. Anderson (Ed.), *The Development of Intelligence*. London: University College Press.

Torff, B. & Warburton, E. in press. "Old and New Models of Cognitive Abilities: The Assessment Conundrum." In M. Pearn (Ed.), *Individual Development in Organisations*. London: Wiley.

About This Book

What This Book Offers the Educational Community

A Focus on Children's Assets: A How-to Guide on Applying Multiple Intelligences to Personalize Learning

In eight short chapters, this book guides educators who want to apply Gardner's ideas about multiple intelligences (MI) to assessment and using portfolios. As the first book to *combine* MI theory with portfolio assessment, it offers a framework to directly improve teachers' classroom assessment of diverse individuals. As a sequel to my previous book, *Whose Judgment Counts: Assessing Bilingual Children (K–3)*, this book focuses on better serving *all* children, not only bilingual and special education students. Overall, it offers a collection of teacher-proven strategies to *best* assess and teach *all* students.

Short, Practical, Classroom-Based Content on Implementing Portfolios

Each chapter contains stories from highly effective school leaders and teachers that illustrate how they use MI to help them understand their students as individuals, and how they design portfolios to personalize teaching and learning. Building and sustaining a whole-school portfolio culture is described by Lynn F. Stuart, a principal in the Cambridge, MA Public Schools, who was the architect of assessment reform for her community. Three chapters offer stories of Cambridge teachers' portfolio systems (grades 1, 2, 5, 6, 7, and 8) designed to better meet the diverse learning needs of all students, including those with bilingual and special education needs. MI becomes an analytic tool for teachers to create multifaceted curriculum documented in portfolios. Portfolios as collections of student work, therefore, become a strong assessment tool and *a window into the learner's mind.*

Useful CD with Sample Student Portfolios and Commentary

A companion CD comes with the book to help readers see and hear how teachers and students use portfolios as celebration and documentation of their learning. The CD shows examples of how to collect, select, and reflect on student work across grade levels (K–8) chronicled from the Cambridgeport School.

About the Author

My interest in multiple intelligences, and in better assessment and teaching practices, comes from my experience as a teacher and special educator. For nineteen years it was my responsibility, as a special educator, to evaluate and then design programs for children from many linguistic and learning backgrounds. I found that standardized tests alone, given their limitations in reliability and validity, do not give sufficient information about a child's individual potential.

After reading Gardner's *Frames of Mind* and learning about the theory of multiple intelligences, I realized that because these tests were based on a theory of a single intelligence I was only gathering data on a small piece of a child's capabilities. I began collecting more data about each child, including observations, teacher reports, parent interviews, and research on child rearing practices. After carefully examining classroom work samples, I began to see that many children who appeared disabled in certain areas—such as writing and spelling—were actually gifted in other areas, such as mathematics, arts, interpersonal skills, or athletics.

I found that by using this wider lens to look at the whole child to identify potential strengths I could address weaknesses.

For example, art, writing, or the computer could help some children learn letters and sounds. Using a wider lens for assessing a child and building a portfolio of his or her work was an essential step to take before appropriate programming and curricular planning could begin.

Using grant monies, I began working with educators from the Chelsea, Boston, and Somerville schools to create and refine an early screening portfolio program to better assess Limited English Proficient (LEP) children's needs for special education. In these systems, most linguistically different children had been failing preschool screening tests and were often eventually placed in special education. The addition of observations, art and play samples, teacher reports, parent interviews, and behavioral checklists provided substantial information about these children which helped teams to program and plan for their learning needs. Often, children did not have the language abilities but *did* have the learning abilities to be mainstreamed even though they "test" poorly. These portfolios became a more accurate assessment of a young child and played a key role in decreasing referrals for special education and increasing programming in bilingual or inclusionary settings. Two key themes emerged related to the assessment of diverse learners:

1. understanding the complexity of a child's language, culture and learning;
2. using multiple formats of assessment and instruction to reach diverse learners.

Both US and international studies (Stefanakis 1991, 1993) pointed to the need for multiple forms of assessment and instruction for young children for language and literacy learning. All children have multiple intelligences and it is our job as educators to use their capabilities, not disabilities, to become more effective teachers.

Rationale: Why Focus Attention on Multiple Intelligences and Portfolios?

For the past twelve years, I have guided teachers to carefully observe children, and gather their work to better understand how they are "smart" or "intelligent" and how they best learn. I ask teachers to use portfolios to study a child, which includes observing the child and gathering cultural and family background information. Collecting work samples from learning activities allows them to consider the student in regard to several of Gardner's intelligences. Teachers can then reflect more deeply on their work to create a more personalized and effective program for each child.

Overview of the Book: Its Contents, Graphics, and Accompanying CD

Chapter 1 begins by offering readers a basic introduction to multiple intelligences theory and its applications, using the most current information about the eight intelligences. It introduces the idea of assessment as sitting beside the learner, and suggests that the process of assessment is based on celebrating and documenting students' work. Using student stories and graphics, it suggests that teaching and learning is about figuring out how each individual is smart (profiling) (Gardner 1993, 1997). All students have all of the intelligences, yet each has a distinct profile; teachers need to understand this if they are to teach effectively to individual strengths. I clarify that MI should not be used as a way to label students, but as an analytic tool to understand the unique learning profile of individuals, as evident in portfolios of their work. A profile does not mean the quantification or description of individual intelligence but a way of looking at an array of abilities.

Chapter 2 provides a framework for designing a portfolio assessment system, based on MI theory, as a way to focus on seeing the whole child. Portfolios offer the teacher a window into the learner's mind and a format for tapping into each learner's strengths; a sample portfolio illustrates how to create a profile of each learner by looking at collections of student work, gathered from best-practice teachers in Cambridge. The portfolio also serves as a tool for the teacher to reflect on this student's needs and then design appropriate curricular innovations to address them. Portfolios at different grade levels are presented on the CD as an appendix to this and the remaining chapters.

Chapters 3 through 6 chronicle the experiences of Lynn F. Stuart, principal of the Cambridgeport School, and her teachers Bela Bhasin, Sarah Fiarman, and Jill Harrison Berg, and provide real-life examples of portfolio work, which are also featured on the CD. In Chapters 3, 5, and 6, teacher colleagues from the Cambridgeport School describe how portfolios of student work help them apply the theory of multiple intelligences to individuals.

The accompanying CD delivers an interactive application: The reader can read the book and simultaneously look at a student's portfolio. Material that could not fit in the book—including graphics, samples of student work, teacher-made portfolio resources—can help readers see how portfolios can help become a window into the learner's mind.

Chapter 3 offers the story of Bela, a primary teacher (grades 1 and 2), describing how portfolios help her learn from students, including those who are bilingual and have special needs. It includes her schedule for the day with built-in times to observe, keep track, and document student learning. This chapter addresses the challenges of portfolio management for early elementary grades.

In Chapters 4 and 7, Lynn F. Stuart, the principal who developed a whole-school portfolio culture at the Cambridgeport School, provides the vital context for how this work developed over time. As a true instructional leader with a vision, she describes the school's journey into becoming a collaborative culture focused on teaching, learning, and assessment.

Chapters 5 and 6 contain portfolio design work from Sarah and Jill working at upper elementary and middle-school levels (grades 5–6 and grades 7–8), where teachers must document the whole child and their skills in language arts, math, science, and social studies. The chapters describe portfolio systems developed to encourage older students to take more responsibility and ownership of the process. In Chapter 6, Jill, a middle-school teacher, working in grades 7–8, presents her format for collecting, selecting, and reflecting on student work to make learning visible to parents, teachers, and students. The design and use of portfolios for graduation, including student presentations of their accomplishments throughout elementary school, is featured in this chapter and on the CD as a model of accountability for middle-school practitioners.

Chapter 8 summarizes some the key lessons learned by teachers and offers a road map for practitioners to use in thinking, planning, and revising their classroom assessment practices. It concludes by suggesting to teachers that elementary classrooms can become laboratories for examining students' work from portfolios, to design learning experiences that tap into the interests of individuals. It further suggests ways to use portfolios that are compatible with the standards and requirements of a public school district assessment system. In conclusion, it suggests alternatives for teachers to use in developing comprehensive assessment systems using portfolios, and outlines a format for future training of school personnel to use the theory of multiple intelligences in portfolio work.

Rationale: Why Apply Multiple Intelligences and Portfolios to Reach All Children?

The Benefits for Teachers, Administrators, Special Educators, and Parents

Multiple intelligences theory offers a way to better educate *all* children, including those with bilingual or special needs. This theory, developed by Gardner and implemented by others, recognizes that students come to knowledge and understanding through various avenues. Each student has a unique set of abilities, but we do not approach the teaching task with a collection of strategies to accommodate their individuality. Not all students will demonstrate their highest potential in the traditional "lecture and take notes" classroom. Multiple intelligences theory suggests that students whose strengths are not in the linguistic or logical-mathematical realm may still have an opportunity to succeed if they are taught differently.

Adapting the theory of multiple intelligences for assessment forces educators to look at each child's learning needs. By looking at each need across a variety of domains, teachers can better focus on their strengths and find specific ways to better engage them in the content they are teaching. Multiple intelligence theory honors and embraces children's diversity. This is crucial in today's schools.

Not only does applying the theory of MI help all children succeed; ideally it also asks instructors to expand their knowledge base and focus on the true art of teaching and learning. Multiple intelligence theory, according to Thomas Armstrong (1994, 11), helps teachers expand their teaching repertoire for reaching an even wider and more diverse range of learners.

MI theory does not advocate abandoning traditional models of education. Rather it legitimizes methods of instruction that might otherwise be considered more *progressive, experiential,* and *active.* If some students learn best by moving, doing, or working with others, then it suggests educators allow these children to demonstrate their aptitudes in the arts, music, theater, interpersonal relations, and athletics in the course of daily instruction practices.

Applications for School Communities: School Leaders, Teachers, and Parents

For the last six years I have been actively engaged in helping teachers, teacher educators, and school leaders understand MI and portfolios and use them in their schools to better serve linguistic minority and special education students in the Boston area. For three years, I worked with the state of Massachusetts Project Zero Network to implement schoolwide portfolio assessment in thirteen model schools. Drawing directly from this work, I focus on the Cambridgeport School and its principal, Lynn F. Stuart, and her teachers and students. They all are characters in this story of portfolio development. Not all teachers can work with teams from Project Zero to understand MI and its implications for adapting curriculum and assessment practices. As I worked with teachers in the Boston area, they repeatedly asked for a simpler, more hands-on guide to implementing MI-based portfolios. This book serves as a "how-to" guide for school leaders, teachers, and potentially even school communities, including parents.

Chapter 1

Multiple Intelligences: A Theory Applied to Learning

Multiple Intelligences: Applied to Individual Learners

Understanding what individual children *do* know, rather than what they *do not* know, has been a challenge for many generations of educators. This challenge is an integral part of any serious attempt to teach a child. Yet, daily life in classrooms rarely focuses on discovering the *full capabilitites* of each individual. Rarely are children assessed as individuals with a unique profile of intelligences.

The lack of a comprehensive assessment process that understands students as individuals is not because of the lack of a theoretical base. In *Frames of Mind*, Howard Gardner (1983, 1993) offers his theory of multiple intelligences (MI): that culture, language, and environment all influence how an individual's intelligence is expressed. He sees *intelligence* as taking three forms: the ability to solve real-life problems, to find and create problems, and to offer a product or a service that is valued in at least one culture (1983).

More recently, Gardner (1999) has said that individuals have at least eight intelligences: linguistic, logical-mathematical, visual-spatial, musical, bodily-kinesthetic, interpersonal, intrapersonal, and the newest naturalistic intelligence, with distinguishing characteristics (as shown in Figure 1–1). Recently Gardner has also hypothesized about an existential intelligence, which refers to the human desire to understand and pursue the ultimate questions and meanings of life.

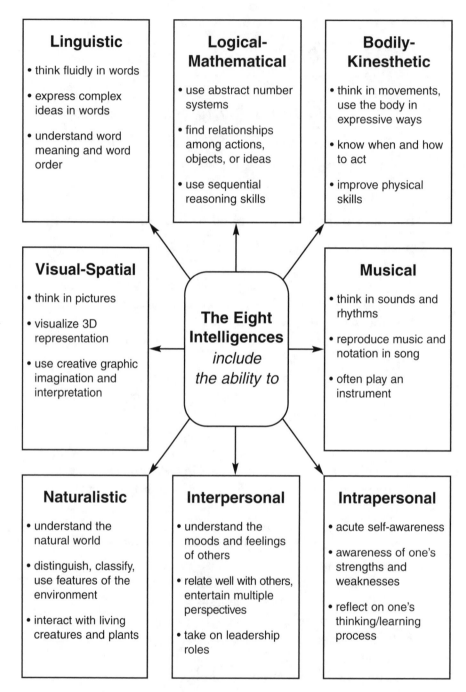

Figure 1–1: *The Eight Intelligences*

Multiple Intelligences or MI offers (educators) insight into the human mind, its abilities, and its development that teachers can understand and use professionally to understand individuals and to better teach all students including those who may be difficult to reach (Armstrong 1999).

According to Gardner (1983), intelligence involves a process of problem solving, problem finding, and contributing to community, which is particularly relevant to daily lives in classrooms. Gardner's definition moves away from a quantifiable number on a linguistic or mathematical test and suggests to teachers that "examining intelligent behaviors" is to document the full range of a student's capabilities. This theory opens the door for educators and parents to appreciate diverse value systems and behaviors, so important to our growing diverse student population.

As Lynn F. Stuart, a colleague and leader in the Cambridge schools suggests, schools may need to retool their view of single intelligence:

> Schools tend to reflect the conventional viewpoint of intelligence as a score on an IQ test. However, in the last twenty years a theoretical revolution has altered the understanding of intelligence dramatically. Intelligence has become plural, yet schools tend to persist in teaching to and testing a singular linguistic or mathematical intelligence. The very people who are responsible for the intellectual development and preparedness of our nation's students for work and citizenship need new bridges between theories of human intelligence and life in the classroom where students learn.

Applying the theory of multiple intelligences suggests acknowledging that all individuals have at least eight intelligences, many of which may not be visible in traditional classroom activities, so focused on linguistic and mathematical intelligences. Applying MI theory to classroom practice begins with teachers shifting from a notion of measuring a single set of intelligence and narrowly defined evidence of student learning, to a new notion of understanding each individual's profile of multiple intelligences. Therefore, teachers need to think about *how* each child is smart, using MI theory as an analytic tool to guide their individual observations and documentation

Key Points—Applying Multiple Intelligences

1. All learners have all eight intelligences. They are combined as channels for learning, not ways to label student abilities.
2. The multiple intelligences are underlying information processing systems that can only be inferred from what children do.
3. Multiple intelligences are combined uniquely in each learner as a profile; they are not seen separately.
4. Individuals have unique profiles based on all of the multiple intelligences; areas of strength can become ways to address areas of weakness (bridging).

of students' learning. As the Campbells (1999) further explain:

> Lack of formal education about human intelligence has left teachers to create their own theories of mind. As Howard Gardner (1991) explains in *The Unschooled Mind*, both adults and children generate personal theories to explain their experiences and perceptions . . . teachers are not immune from theory generating. To make sense of individual students' learning capabilities they encounter, they construct scripts (or profiles) about the intelligence of those in their charge. These implicit beliefs can be optimistic or pessimistic, constrictive or expansive.

By making a case for multiple intelligences, Gardner has confirmed the suspicions of educators who deal with a wide range of individual student differences. Gardner's work encourages educators and parents to gather additional information on individuals to better understand and use a wider array of students' capabilities.

Beginnings: Applying Multiple Intelligences to Better Understand Individuals

I believe MI theory offers useful assumptions about learners as individuals, as well as about teaching, learning, and assessment.

Frequently, teachers who have heard or read about Gardner's theory lack any concrete system that translates MI theory into assessment-driven curricular practices. Especially when joined to portfolio assessment, based on collections of student work, multiple intelligences offers a process for bridging the gap between theory and practice.

This book focuses on the challenge of understanding the multiple intelligences of individuals in order to help educators really *teach* every child. As a book designed for practitioners, it suggests how MI theory *and* student portfolios can be applied to better understand the uniqueness of learners and their learning. To describe learner-centered classrooms that use portfolios, throughout the book I use stories of children, their teachers, and the daily interactions in school activities. This book also considers how MI theory and portfolios can be used in a whole-school setting.

Welcome to the story of how all students are smart in many ways if we reconsider what *smart* means! The story begins like this . . .

The Poor Learner's Soliloquy

No, I'm not very good in school. This is my second year in the seventh grade and I'm bigger and taller than the other kids are. They like me all right, though, even if I don't say much in the schoolroom, because outside I can tell them how to do lots of things. I don't know why the teachers don't like me. They never have very much. Seems like they don't think you know anything unless you can name the book it comes out of. I've got a lot of books in my room at home—books like *Popular Science Mechanics Encyclopedia*, and the Sears' catalog, but I don't very often just sit down and read them like they make us do in school.

I use my books when I want to find something out, like whenever Mom buys anything second hand I look it up in Sears' first and tell her if she's getting stung or not. I can use the index in a hurry to find the things I want.

I guess I just can't remember names in history. Anyway, this year I've been trying to learn about trucks because my uncle owns three and he says I can drive one when I'm sixteen. I already know the horsepower and number of forward and backward speeds of twenty-six American trucks, some of them diesels. I can spot each make a long way off. It's funny how that diesel works. I started to tell my teacher about it last Wednesday in science class when the pump we were using to make a vacuum in a bell jar got hot, but she said she didn't see what a diesel engine had to do with our experiment on air pressure, so I just kept still. The kids seemed interested, though. I took four of them around to my uncle's garage after school and we saw the mechanic, Gus, tearing a big diesel truck down. Boy, does he know his stuff!

I'm not very good in geography either. They call it economic geography this year. We've been studying the exports and imports of Chile all week but I couldn't tell you what they are. Maybe the reason is I had to miss school yesterday because my uncle took me and his big trailer truck down state about 200 miles and we brought almost 10 tons of stock to the Chicago market.

He had told me where we were going, and I had to figure the highways to take and also the mileage. He didn't do anything but drive and turn where I told him. Was that fun! I sat with a map in my lap and told him to turn south or southeast or in some other direction. We made seven stops and drove over five hundred miles round trip. I'm figuring out what his oil cost and also the wear and tear on the truck—he calls it depreciation—so we'll know how much we made.

I don't do very well in school arithmetic, either. Seems I just can't keep my mind on the problems. We had one the other day like this: "If a 57-foot telephone pole falls across a cement highway so that $17\text{-}3/6$ feet extend from one side and $14\text{-}6/17$ feet extend from the other, how wide is the highway?" That seemed to me like an awfully silly way to get the width of a highway. I didn't even try to answer it because it didn't say whether the pole had fallen straight across or not.

Dad says I can quit school when I'm fifteen, and I am sort of anxious to because there are a lot of things I want to learn how to

do and, as my uncle says, I'm not getting any younger. I really wonder why no one thinks I could be smarter if school was a different place?
—Adapted from S. Covey, *Childhood Education*, 1944

As many teachers who work with a variety of students know, it is not easy to reach every individual. Who are the students we consider smart? What happens to students who think they are not smart, whose talent schools may not see?

According to Gardner's definition, how is this student intelligent? What does this Poor Learner's Soliloquy suggest to educators about schools?

Is it really that this student is not smart and cannot pass the courses, meet the grades, or get the diploma? According to the notion of one intelligence, some students are smart and the others are not smart. Teachers typically decide who is smart and not so smart according to a few intelligences as echoed in the Poor Learner's Soliloquy. What about the poor learner's kinesthetic, visual-spatial, logical-mathematical, bodily-kinesthetic, interpersonal, intrapersonal, and naturalistic intelligence? He can read maps, calculate budgets, raise animals, and describe how a diesel engine works.

According to the MI theory, we need to dramatically shift the way we think about learning and therefore assessing all learners. Teachers should not ask themselves, "is this a smart student?" but "*how* is this student smart?" More important, educators may need to acknowledge the possibility that this student may be very smart—if only he were taught more effectively, in a variety of ways.

For the most part, struggling learners' other talents are seldom verbalized, but even if they are, they may work against a student's life as in the Poor Learner's Soliloquy. If education for all means that no child should be left behind, then applying MI theory to teaching, learning, and assessment is vital to help teachers better teach and succeed with all students, including those who may be difficult to teach.

Shifting Beliefs: From Who Is Smart? to How Is Each One Smart?

Applying MI theory means focusing on the uniqueness of the individual learner. Specifically, teachers might have to look more closely at those learners who are not learning in the typical ways teachers expect them to learn. To apply MI theory, teachers must first examine their deep beliefs about individual learners and learning, given what researchers have found. This may suggest abandoning beliefs about whether a single intelligence can measure "how smart a student is." It suggests shifting to Gardner's (1983, 1993) beliefs that all children are smart—in different ways. Simply put, it means understanding that teaching and learning means figuring out or assessing *how each individual is smart*, and using this information to actively engage that individual in a multifaceted learning process.

Jacob, a first grade student, is a good example of how a teacher can use MI theory as a lens to look at samples of student work (in a portfolio) and observe that student at work over time (in classroom observations) to change his/her approach and better address the child's learning challenges. He has a very difficult time sitting still and concentrating when lessons are presented orally. He also struggles with his written work and seems to have a writer's block during every writing period. However, when Jacob is in the block or LEGO area, he can concentrate for hours on the structures he builds. When his teacher asks him about his structures, he immediately tells her the elaborate, detailed stories he is developing through his construction activities. For Jacob, the entry point to *writing* his stories begins with using areas of strength: his visual-spatial, logical-mathematical, and bodily-kinesthetic intelligences. Once his teacher recognized these talents, she was able to capture his stories by engaging him in discussion about his buildings, asking him first to draw his constructions and then write about them in stories.

An older student, Genet, seemed extremely disorganized in doing assignments and especially had trouble surviving in her math class. She constantly struggled with basic operations, with problem-solving and written assignments. On the other hand, she was very clearly artistic as evident in her student work collections. Further, she was a strong navigator and play-maker for the girls' soccer team. Her teachers, identifying her strengths in visual-spatial abilities, interpersonal, and bodily-kinesthetic intelligence, began to teach her to use graphic organizers and thinking maps. These strategies help her organize her assignments, outline mathematical operations, and approach written problem solving. Genet's strength areas along with her social skills became a bridge for her to better address her weaknesses.

For teachers using MI, teaching becomes a process of understanding the multiple intelligences of a class of individuals, and using this information to make daily decisions about *what to teach* and *how to teach*. For teachers who seek to reach every child, it is not merely a question of *what* to teach to the group, but *how* to teach the material; often with a choice of activities, in ways that can tap into the multiple intelligences of learners. A starting point for many teachers is to use portfolios as collections of student work, which become a tool to begin the process of applying MI theory to improve teaching practices. This kind of assessment is also the key to changing deeply held beliefs and practices. Portfolios offer a way to better understand a learner by documenting the process and the products of their learning. Portfolios help teachers build an MI profile of that learner. Student work, collected and analyzed, invites consideration of all the ways learners learn.

Assessment Means *Sitting Beside* the Learner

Assessing an individual child requires first understanding the definition of *assessment*. The word *assess* comes from the Latin *assidere*, which means *to sit beside*. Literally then, *to assess* means to *sit beside the learner*. I believe that this position—beside a child—is the best way to actively understand that individual. This makes assessing a learning experience for the teacher who gathers information from learners to see their unique capabilities, not disabilities. When teachers sit next to, rather than in front of students and ask them about their classroom products, they begin to show that they care to know *how* an individual student has made meaning out of an assignment or a project. The ongoing conversations between students and teachers about the work they create together in the classroom offer them both a chance to better understand their interactive learning process.

To carefully assess an individual, using the notion of multiple intelligences as an analytic tool, is a complex and multifaceted process (Stefanakis 1998) involving observation, documentation, and assessment. For classroom teachers, this begins by shifting from a position of power, from being in front of or above the learner, to sitting beside the learner to see the unique interactions of individuals as they learn. I chose these phrases carefully because each one has a significant image to convey. When teacher and student sit beside one another to look into portfolios, they make the first subtle but significant shift in the assessment process.

The Power in Portfolios: A Way to Sit Beside Each Learner

Imagine a classroom in which grading is based on evidence of learning that is visible in student work over time: selected samples of writing, math, science, and social studies; project work; art; journals, quizzes, tests, or other classroom activities. Imagine a classroom in which teachers and students regularly sit beside one another to assess these collections of student work and to define the next steps in their teaching and learning process. Imagine a class in which teachers regularly look at students' work and look at how students do that work to better understand the multiple intelligences (Gardner 1983) of these individuals. This ongoing practice of examining daily classroom work allows teachers and students to be *co-learners*, to discover, to use, and to build on an individual child's abilities.

Teachers and students in these classrooms use portfolios, or

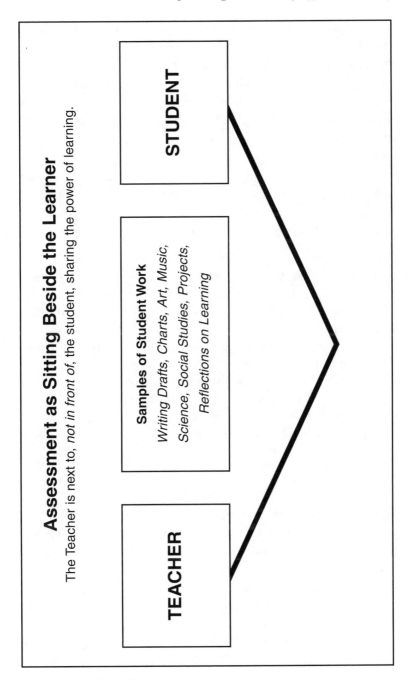

Figure 1–2: *Assessment as Sitting Beside the Learner*

collections of student work, to guide their interactions related to teaching, learning, and assessment. Portfolios are a powerful tool that can help teachers in their efforts to reach and teach every child, including those who are bilingual or may have special needs. To understand the power of portfolios as an assessment tool, I suggest we look at expert teachers and listen to what they say about how they assess the learners in their classrooms.

Eric Johnson, a skilled third-grade teacher in an urban school, keeps track of his students' individual progress by collecting their work in portfolios. For Eric these collections are evidence of what his students care about and are excited to learn; they document student growth.

> I keep a portfolio of the student's writing, art, math, and other things they make. What they want to save is important, so I ask them to help me select the work we keep. To me, this is the data on a child.
>
> Looking at their work and how it is made helps me see how they are smart. I observe when the child is creating a piece of work, then I listen to what the child says about the work. I try to make a note of what they are telling me about the work and themselves—what excites them as they learn.
>
> This data—the work and how it is created—helps me build a profile on each child. Students' work is what I use to know better what they know and how to help them learn.

Thus Eric sees that each student's work (the product) and how it is created (the process) become data on a child. It helps him as a teacher see *how* each child is smart and *how* to develop a profile of the individual learner. Using MI theory as an analytic tool, Eric looks at student work over time to gather information about each student's strengths, whether she or he is mathematical, visual-spatial, linguistic, bodily-kinesthetic, musical, interpersonal, intrapersonal, or naturalistic. The written, artistic, and graphic pieces of a project can help Eric infer something about a child's visual-spatial, bodily-kinesthetic, logical-mathematical, and even interpersonal abilitites. For teachers like Eric, student work becomes a window into under-standing more about the multiple intelligences of a child: It pro-vides evidence of a collection of performances in the arts, in sports, in language, in mathematics, or in self-understanding.

Eric explains:

> I make time to sit beside each of my students to watch and note what they do. Then I sit beside them, not just in front of them, as often as I can to look at their portfolio of work. I do this by focus-ing on two or three students a day.
>
> I ask them questions about what pieces mean to them. I feel like these two practices, looking at them and looking at their work, helps me know each of them as an individuals and find ways to use their abilities, not disabilities, in the activities we do.

When a teacher like Eric sits beside a student, periodically looking at her work and listening to her reflections, he understands more about how that individual thinks and learns (Stefanakis 1998). Eric's profile on each student helps him think, plan, and create a collection of classroom activities to address each child's interests and abilities.

But it is not only the teacher who benefits from looking at student work in a portfolio. The fact that a teacher regularly cares enough to examine an individual student's work and talk to her about it means a lot to that learner. This makes curricu-lum building a shared experience for the teacher and for the student—guided both by what teacher and student want to know and want to learn.

How Portfolios Help Teachers Become Researchers of Individuals

Knowing the individual passions of the students in a classroom can make teaching and learning a very different experience for both teacher and learner. Using the idea of *sitting beside* the learner as an assessment process, the teacher begins by observ-ing the student collecting and documenting student work to create the profile. Although many excellent teachers are careful observers of their students, their good intentions about keeping notes and records are hard to maintain.

One simple solution is to put a piece of that work back on the shoulders of the students. They can collect, select, and reflect on their work, noting pieces that they see as challenging and as breakthroughs in learning. This reflective process becomes part of the daily classroom routine.

How might this happen? Collections of student work, captured in a portfolio, become a tool for teachers and students to see evidence of growth over time. Students date their work, keep all the drafts, select representative pieces, and reflect on them for ten minutes of daily portfolio time. Teachers use student work to share the evidence of their accomplishments, periodically finding five to ten minutes to sit beside a child to listen to reflections on it. These interactions begin to change the power relationship between student and teacher, as they talk about the evidence of learning evident in a student's work. These conferences help the teacher to examine the student's work in relation to district or state standards and to personalize goals for that student. Teachers learn from their student's work about the process and the product of daily classroom activitites.

Portfolios: The Window into the Learner's Mind and Capabilities

How does a teacher use student work in a portfolio to create a profile of the learner and then personalize the learning process? To illustrate a teacher's process of thinking by using student work, I devote the rest of this chapter to examining Mai-Mai's portfolio.

Mai-Mai's teacher Bela collected many examples of classroom work from the year, but she and Mai-Mai selected only about ten to twelve pieces to keep. These work samples become the documentation that helps Bela create an MI profile of Mai-Mai as a learner. Mai-Mai's portfolio contained a diverse set of work samples: her daily journal writing, literacy projects, math activities, drawings, book-making, and science experiments.

How Does a Teacher Create an MI Profile?

To create a profile of this learner, Bela started by sorting Mai-Mai's work by date, putting a few key pieces of each quarter's products in chronological order. At least once a month Mai-Mai and Bela discussed which pieces to save. This gave her periodic samples of Mai-Mai's work and reflections as evidence of her growth over time. As a management strategy, Bela, like Eric, finds talking to two students a day is a manageable way to gather data to create profiles of twenty-four students. At each parent conference, Bela shared samples of student work with Mai-Mai's family. Together, parents and teachers brainstormed about how to personalize Mai-Mai's learning activities, at home and at school, to build on her strengths and address areas of weakness.

Next, Bela used MI theory to examine work samples from Mai-Mai's portfolio, considering in each piece of work what skills were addressed in specific assignments. She listened to Mai-Mai's tapes of reading aloud recorded from September, November, February, and June. As she looked at Mai-Mai's collection of work, her drawings, stories, journal writing, and math, themes and patterns in her work emerge. Bela's reflections, inferred from the portfolio collection, help her build an MI profile of Mai-Mai:

- Mai-Mai's writing and art show a keen awareness of her visual environment and the people in it. This is evident repeatedly in her family and people drawing, her journal entries, and especially in her Who Am I? Booklet. From samples Bela can infer that Mai-Mai seems to have strengths in visual-spatial, bodily-kinesthetic, and interpersonal intelligences.
- Mai-Mai is developing large motor movements in cutting and pasting and improving in her autobiographical personal timeline, butterfly project, and accompanying reflections. Yet earlier handwriting samples capture her

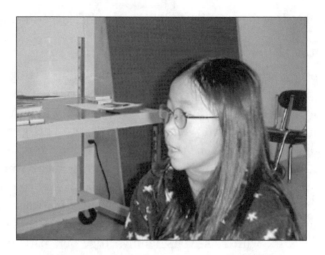

Figure 1–3: *Mai-Mai*

Figure 1–4: *Samples of Mai-Mai's portfolio. View the whole portfolio on the CD–ROM.*

initial struggle with the physical act of making letters and symbols. Samples of writing from March to June are evidence of her eventual growth in this area over the year. From project samples, Bela can infer something about Mai-Mai's challenges in areas of bodily-kinesthetic, visual-spatial, and intrapersonal intelligences.

- Comparing portfolio drawings and writing samples shows emerging themes and patterns. Mai-Mai's work samples show marked differences in the two bodily-kinesthetic abilities of fine and large motor movements. Her written work from September to January shows steady growth in letter formation and the use of written conventions. This also suggests that teaching activities in the classroom are probably addressing her needs. What can be inferred from a collection of student work is that there is a pattern of strength in visual-spatial, bodily-kinesthetic, and inter-personal intelligences.

- Since English is not her first language but Chinese is, language development is initially a challenge for Mai-Mai. Over time, her teacher observed Mai-Mai's language skills indirectly by listening to reading tapes and directly by observing paired reading in the classroom. Examining Mai-Mai's paired reading journal and story writing shows her basic ideas are expressed. In many of these written pieces from her grade 1 portfolio it is often hard to decode what Mai-Mai is trying to say on paper. Her teacher made some inferences about Mai-Mai's linguistic and bodily-kinesthetic intelligences that show great variation over the course of the year. She began to think about how other strengths could be a bridge to challenge areas.

- **An initial MI Profile:** Mai-Mai's pictures and artwork, in general, say more than her words. Later in the year (see January to May portfolio samples), her stories and written pieces are easier to understand. Mai-Mai's portfolio documents growing skills in linguistic areas. Work samples show that she is initially challenged by complex tasks

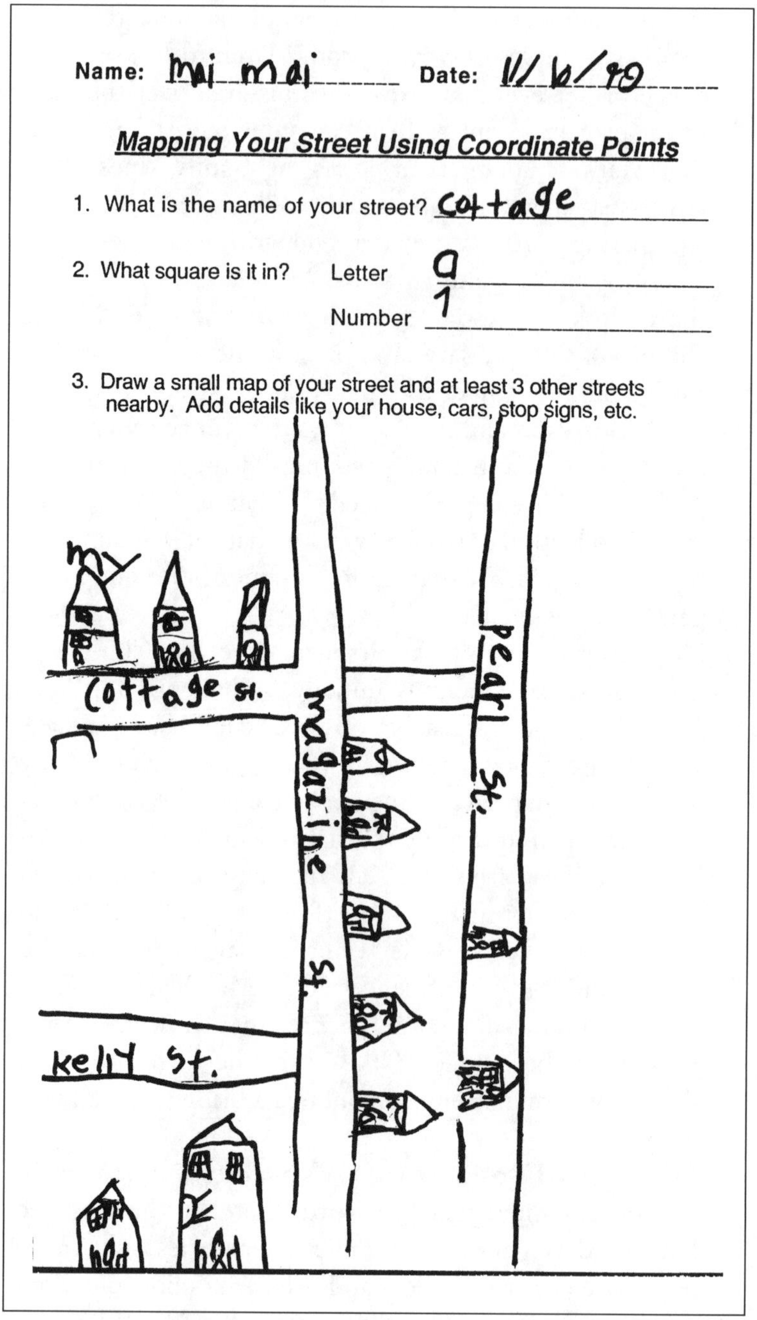

Name: mai mai   **Date:** 11/6/90

Mapping Your Street Using Coordinate Points

1. What is the name of your street? cottage

2. What square is it in?   Letter $\frac{a}{1}$

   Number

3. Draw a small map of your street and at least 3 other streets nearby. Add details like your house, cars, stop signs, etc.

Figure 1–5a: *Mai-Mai's street map*

𝔄 𝔓iece for 𝔐y 𝔓ortfolio

Name **Mai   Mai**   Date **6/8/99**

What did you choose?

steert   map

Why did you choose this piece?

I chose it because my map shows all of the steerts   in the right Places.

What does this piece of work show about your learning?

I learned how to create a map to show where I live.

Figure 1–5b: *Mai-Mai's reflection on why she chose the street map for her portfolio.*

related to the sound-symbol relationship, especially in areas of handwriting and spelling (see work samples in Figure 1–6).

In order to utilize Mai-Mai's visual-spatial, bodily-kinesthetic, and interpersonal strengths as a bridge to address linguistic and other kinesthetic (large motor) issues, her teacher referred her to the Reading Recovery teacher to get focused attention

---

Reading Log (1st grade)

Title(s) of the book(s): the Great,

enormous hamburger

Today's Date: 10/23/98

One comment I have about what I read today is.. I Lik to

they Put on the fad.

I ordo nat lik hamlnburger.

Reading Log (2nd grade)

Today's Date: 3/17/99

Title of the Book: Angel child, Dragon

Author: Michele Surat   Pages read: 0 to

One comment I have about what I read today is...

I did't like the doy
how teased ut becaUse
he hurt her feelings, He
stop when the princi pal came.

Figure 1–6a: *Mai-Mai's reading logs showing a comparison between 1998 and 1999.*

on the sound-symbol relationship and on writing using spelling using cards, drawings, and graphic tools. In the classroom, Mai-Mai's teacher found specific times to engage her in written language activities and to observe her growth. She sat beside this learner, talking with Mai-Mai about her samples of writing during monthly portfolio conferences. Bela used multiple intelligences and portfolios to help personalize the instructional plan for her. Mai-Mai's collection of student work deepened Bela's understanding of her as an individual student which became vital information that could be used to address her learning needs. Creating an MI profile by combining observations and portfolio documentation helped Bela better know how to teach Mai-Mai and others with learning challenges.

Reaching Every Child Personally: Creating a Profile and a Portfolio

Mai-Mai's portfolios offer a means for teacher and learner to regularly sit beside one another to look at collections of student work. This teacher and student regularly looked at a single piece

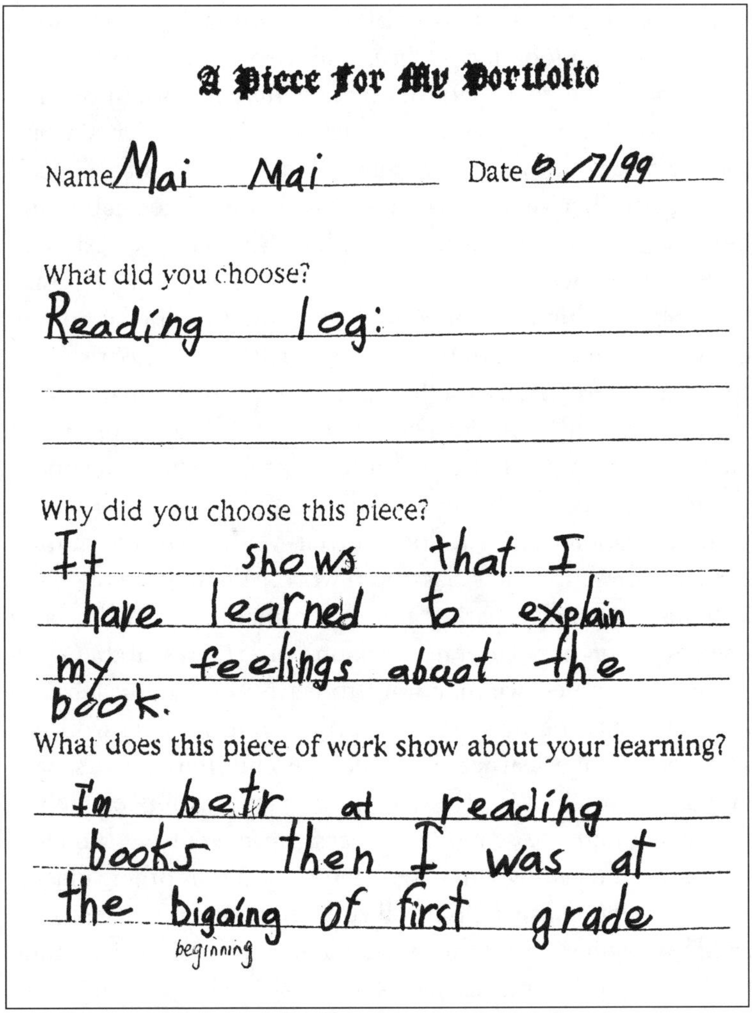

A Piece for My Portfolio

Name **Mai Mai**   Date **6/7/99**

What did you choose?

Reading log:

_____

_____

Why did you choose this piece?

It shows that I have learned to explain my feelings about the book.

What does this piece of work show about your learning?

I'm betr at reading books then I was at the bigaing of first grade

beginning

Figure 1–6b: *Mai-Mai's reflection on why she chose to add the reading logs to her portfolio.*

of work or collection of work, discussed how it was created, evaluating what it showed, and then jointly defined how to make the work better. Assessment in this way became a learning experience for the teacher *and* for the learner as they examined the collection of student work.

Simply, the connection between MI and portfolios begins by examining a collection of student work to gather data on the learner. Using the framework of MI theory as an analytic tool, the teacher can look for patterns and themes in individual student work. The goal is not to identify student work in relation to individual intelligences. As a teacher looks at students' work, she considers the varying combinations of linguistic, logical-mathematical, visual-spatial, musical, bodily-kinesthetic, and interpersonal abilities of the individual. She sees the variety of ways that learners approach different tasks. The teacher combines observation and portfolio documentation to take note of the whole child—as a linguist, as an artist, as a scientist, as a cooperative learner, as a reflective learner, and as a mathematician. Every child's performance and work samples present a picture of strength, but each piece helps a teacher infer more about the profile of the individual's multiple intelligences.

Take a moment now to look at Mai-Mai's portfolio samples as a lens to examine her classroom work. What do we observe? Perhaps it's time to gather more information about her as a scientist given her elaborate work on butterfly research. Given her work samples, we may want to learn more about her as a mathematician because we have little about her data work, or as a cooperative learner. How do the children she sits with interact with her? Can classroom interviews with peers help?

Throughout the schooling process, teachers have the daily challenge of teaching language, literacy, and four other subjects while simultaneously helping all children learn how to learn. As children begin their journey in elementary school, this is a time for both parents and teachers to discover who a child is and how that child learns. These are ideal years for teachers and parents to understand more about the multiple intelligences of individual learners and to use portfolios as a guide in this process. Portfolios can tell the *story of learning*, helping to document the products and processes of its daily course. Looking at students' work in portfolios can help teachers, parents, and next year's teachers see more about who each student is and use this information to guide their future learning.

In the next chapters, I present several portraits of practice in which teachers and others describe how portfolios help them understand the individuals they teach. Throughout the book we will meet teachers from grades one to eight and their school principal who collaboratively worked to apply MI theory to adapt their curriculum and assessment. As we look more closely at these practitioners' stories, I believe we will see how adapting portfolios as an assessment tool asks teachers to *sit beside* learners on a regular basis, to actively reflect on the student work, which helps them know their learners and how to best teach them. Portfolios invite teachers to take stock and see if the work they ask students to do is worthwhile, and whether it is helping students gain the skills they need. When teachers look at student work to see how they are achieving standards, and how students' interests match their teaching, everyone is working on improvment. This frequent and vital interaction—looking at student work—allows teachers and students to be co-learners and to collaboratively set goals, to use individuals' strengths as a bridge to address weaknesses. These are the individuals whose judgments count in evaluating the power of portfolios as a tool to improve teaching and learning. Stephanie Marshall (Stefanakis 1998) reminds us:

> Assessment is not an end in itself. It is a process that facilitates appropriate instructional decisions by providing information on two fundamental questions:
>
> • How are *we* (teacher and learner) doing?
> • How can *we* (teacher and learner) do better?

Why Use Portfolios?

- Because students invest their work with meaning, understanding, and purpose—when they feel their work is considered for those qualities.
- Because looking at things that students make—pictures, stories, journals, maps, projects—provides a view into the individual and the learning environment.
- Because a longitudinal view of children's work provides a picture and a profile of growth, progress, and continuity over time.
- Because portfolios provide assessment based on evidence of students' efforts, not a list of test scores.

Chapter 2

A Window into the Learner's Multiple Intelligences

An optimal learning environment is a classroom where the teacher's job is to assess each individual child, to see "how he or she is smart," and to use students' strengths as a catalyst to understanding new, more complex, learning tasks.

(Eric Johnson)

When we recall a favorite teacher, suprisingly it may well be the one who tapped into our multiple intelligences. This was the teacher who knew each of us as an individual, and made us feel *smart*, perhaps in a variety of ways. Imagine Mrs. Penwarden, that sixth-grade teacher who let you work in groups to learn about the Roman Empire through personally designed projects about being a Roman. She let students *become* Romans through performances and role-plays: dressing in togas, using Roman numerals for math, and creating a to-scale replica of a coliseum. She even let teams build chariots out of old shopping carts and race them on the school grounds to reenact Roman life. As a culminating experience, the classroom became a Roman forum and marketplace, complete with foods and wares from ancient times. Science study focused on how weather affected peoples' lives during that time, and the impact of the erupting volcano on the city of Pompeii. There were multiple entry points to the curriculum on Rome and many ways that the unit study was assessed.

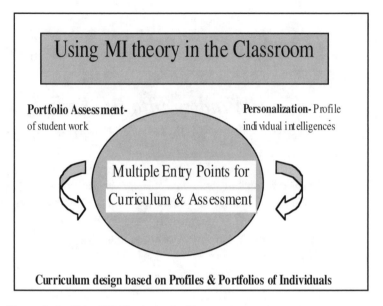

Figure 2–1: *Using MI Theory in the Classroom*

Teachers As Researchers of Individuals: Engaging Diverse Learners

These are the kinds of learning experiences that many people, regardless of their age, recall and describe as examples of deep understanding and engagement in a topic or unit of study. This same teacher probably reveled in the talents of children and their unique ways of expressing ideas or of making things. She left the single course textbook to the side and tried to bring learning alive by listening to the interests of individuals in the classroom. This teacher was creating an environment to nurture the multiple intelligences of individual students: noting those who displayed strengths as naturalists, artists, musicians, athletes, scientists, mathematicians, or whatever they might become.

Each of these unique interests was captured somewhere in the ongoing study of Roman life and times. The unit of study was designed to provide choices or multiple entry points to the topic for the diverse group of learners in the classroom. Mrs.

Penwarden extended this philosophy into her teaching approach by encouraging students to demonstrate their learning in any number of formats: using art, drama, simulations, science experiments, or math applications. Like others who apply the theory of multiple intelligences to design curriculum, she used diverse ways of gathering and expressing ideas and allowed students to exhibit them in multiple formats. Figure 2–2, A Planning Framework and Map, shows some of the activities she used to apply MI theory to build this unit plan. The eight intelligences are abbreviated as follows in the figure: L=Linguistic, VS=Visual-Spatial, LM=Logical-Mathematical, BK=Bodily-Kinesthetic, N=Naturalistic, M=Musical, I=Interpersonal, IP=Intrapersonal.

As they observe, listen, and talk to the collection of students in their classes, teachers like Mrs. Penwarden become researchers of individuals. They try to discover a personal interest in each student and tie it to the topic of life in Roman times. By personalizing the learning experience, Mrs. Penwarden uses observations to understand her students' interests in relation to life in Roman times. She could then work with individual students to design personalized projects around their interests. For example, she observed Adam drawing patterns on his paper and hypothesized that he might be inclined to study the art and symbols of ancient Rome. Giving him a way to use his artistic capabilities in a personalized project, she ignited a new spark for this student in understanding Roman times. Another classmate, Evan, who was interested in Roman art and activities, which drew on visual-spatial, linguistic, and interpersonal intelligences, could join Adam in a personally designed project.

Jane, a student Mrs. Penwarden observed to have a compelling interest in the natural sciences, began to study the physical changes in the earth before and after the eruption of Mt. Vesuvius. After doing her own research, Jane could go on to study the impact of the eruption on Pompeii with others in her group. Jane examined the people and places around that

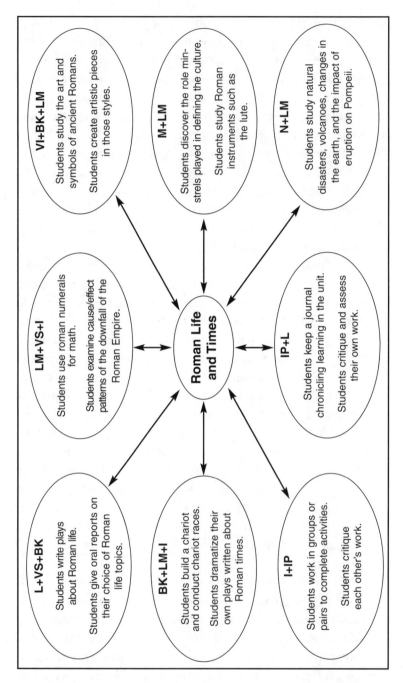

Figure 2–2: *How Do People Live in Roman Times? A Planning Framework and Map*

natural disaster, drawing on her strengths in naturalistic, bodily-kinesthetic, logical-mathematical, and intrapersonal intelligences. The whole class eventually went on to study natural disasters and their effects on the ancient people of Greece and Rome. Threads of history were reenacted as students wrote plays to chronicle how tidal waves and volcanoes hypothetically changed ancient civilizations. They incorporated historic content from their text to make their Roman "dramas" authentic.

Changing the Relationship of Teacher and Student

Ongoing classroom assessment is an art. Through systematically looking at each child's daily work, and listening to what they say, a teacher can learn more about the individual and what he or she really knows and can do. By observing, collecting, and reflecting on student work, Kathleen, a teacher in an inclusion class, creates a profile of the multiple intelligences of individual students in her third grade. Her classroom of twenty-four students in an elementary school in Cambridge, Massachusetts, has four to five students who are bilingual or have disabilities. She has a teacher associate who works with her to offer students support in language and learning areas. Kathleen researches each individual by assessing and sitting beside them to better understand the diversity of her learners. How does Kathleen begin?

Starting a Profile of a Student: Sitting Beside the Learner

Kathleen observes each child and examines their work using MI theory as a lens to consider strengths related to linguistic, logical-mathematical, musical-rhythmic, interpersonal, intrapersonal, visual-spatial, bodily-kinesthetic, and naturalistic intelligences (Gardner 1983, 1993, 1997). Through daily interactions and observations of what children do, she informally assesses individual skills and abilities as evident in student work. She developed a portfolio and profile of Filomena, a bilingual student, to better distinguish a learning problem from a language-acquisition issue:

> The child that comes to mind is Filomena, because of her evaluation records. She had been tested over and over and I read the report and put it aside. It did not teach me what she could do [how she was smart].
>
> I needed to know what she can do, what her work showed, and where to begin to best teach her.
>
> I find out so much more by being with the child and looking at student work than from test reports. From watching her over time and documenting her classwork in a focused collection of samples, I learned that she was having clear difficulty with language that goes beyond being bilingual and beyond any developmental questions. I know there are strengths and there has been progress with her, but it has been a tedious process.

Kathleen uses samples of student work and assumes she will look to see "how Filomena is smart" even though specialists' observations may not indicate this. She begins by sitting beside the learner to discover what she can do. She uses MI theory to look systematically at what this child does well, and where she struggles. Kathleen describes her ongoing observations of Filomena and her examination of work samples from a portfolio:

> In the beginning, I thought that she was only speaking Portuguese at home. I was confused, since she speaks mostly Portuguese with her mother, and her father speaks English. Through her daily journal pictures, I learned that he is not at home that much, so she is basically speaking Portuguese most of the time.
>
> Sometimes I get really frustrated because progress is slow. This is when I start collecting pieces of work that are dated into a portfolio. The work shows me that she is making progress. She is developing in areas of literacy, in the words she prints and recalls,

as her samples show. I have confidence that reading will happen. In the portfolio work I infer she is a capable artist, scientist, cooperative learner, and musician. She may not be reading fluently, but she is capable in many other ways as her project work shows.

By sitting beside her I learned that she can match letters and sounds, although she cannot remember the names of the letters. While collecting daily dictation samples, I found that if I give her a sound to her, she may identify the letter. Yes, she is making progress because we were able to try different strategies based on developing an MI profile.

Kathleen observes, documents, and keeps track of student work to create an MI profile which guides her future programming for Filomena:

I see she knows where to look in the classroom to get help. She uses the visual cues in the environment. Her work shows that she copies from charts or anywhere she can see a word.

I never really thought too much about individual issues until I came to an inclusion class. In here we have such a variety of learners that may not appear to have strengths. The portfolios show they are capable and help us use MI theory to change our teaching.

For Kathleen, multiple intelligences became an analytic tool to guide her ongoing observation and documentation of Filomena's learning. By sitting beside this learner and creating a profile of her strengths in different learning situations, she has found a window into this child's learning. Now she is more prepared to reach this child, and others who may also be a puzzle because of learning differences.

Getting Started: Using Multiple Intelligences to Better Understand Individuals

Applying MI theory means first understanding that all individuals have at least eight intelligences, many of which do not show up in traditional classroom activities, which tend to focus on linguistic and mathematical intelligences. This suggests that teachers shift from a notion of measuring intelligence and student learning to a new notion of understanding individual students' multiple intelligences, by observing and documenting a collection of their work. Portfolios, as collections of work, help teachers to create a profile of student abilities.

Second, to better understand each child's unique intelligence profile requires a shift in the position of power between teacher and learner. Teachers have to redesign learning tasks to allow them to more often sit beside individual learners to see and hear how they best learn. Knowing them better means teaching them better.

This personalization creates a more inclusive learning environment for the individual student, as well as the group of students in the class. Figures 2–3 and 2–4 are examples of tools to assist readers in creating profiles of their students. A student/teacher profiling chart (on the CD-ROM) allows the student to self-assess his or her abilities related to the intelligences and provides space for the teacher to respond with observations and documentation from student work collections. *Additional forms are available on the CD-ROM.*

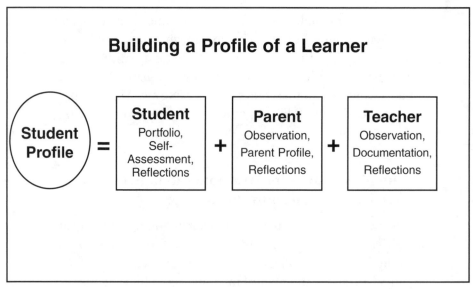

Figure 2–3: *Building a Profile of a Learner*

Seeing Individuals in Their Work—Creating a Student Profile Through Portfolios

How do portfolios really help teachers become researchers of individuals? How can teachers create an environment that allows them to observe, document, and keep track of the work of students, including those who have diverse language and learning needs? Miguel's classroom practices demonstrate how he started using portfolio assessment to define his instructional practice and to differentiate his teaching. Portfolios helped him and others in his school understand the complexity of individual learners' academic, social, cultural, and linguistic backgrounds. Each learner, according to Miguel's philosophy about children and how they learn, is unique and capable. However, social interaction is the key to helping adults and children learn together. Miguel's teaching philosophy is based on a premise that all children like to learn what they are interested in.

Getting Started: Applying Multiple Intelligences to Differentiate Curriculum and Assessment

How does a teacher like Miguel create an environment where MI theory and portfolios are tools of ongoing and regular classroom assessment?

Student work for Miguel becomes evidence of the process and products of his students' learning as well as the guide to improving his teaching.

Miguel's Classroom Design: Student Work Folders Become Portfolios

Miguel, a second-grade teacher in an urban public school, keeps track of individual students' progress by collecting work samples in a portfolio for each child in his class. These portfolios are collections of work that students select to document growth in literacy and other subject areas. Portfolios, for

To be completed in one-on-one interviews (with student) when used with younger students. Older students will be able to complete it themselves.

1 = almost never; 2 = sometimes; 3 = often; 4 = almost always

___ Likes to read
___ Tells stories and jokes well
___ Listens carefully and effectively
___ Has a wide vocabulary—uses words correctly
___ Accurately remembers information
___ Expresses self well in speaking and writing
___ Enjoys tongue twisters, nonsense rhymes, and puns
___ Describes or persuades easily when speaking

___ Identifies patterns and relationships among objects or numbers
___ Calculates numbers quickly, easily, and accurately
___ Enjoys brainteasers or games that require logical thinking
___ Enjoys playing games of strategy
___ Solves problems by reasoning them out
___ Enjoys scientific investigation and experimentation
___ Is organized

___ Enjoys physical activities and/or sports
___ Likes to work with his or her hands
___ Learns best when allowed to touch and manipulate objects
___ Is well coordinated
___ Handles tools skillfully
___ Excels in dance or theatrical performance
___ Mimics others skillfully

___ Plays a musical instrument
___ Remembers melodies and musical pieces easily
___ Frequently chooses to listen to music
___ Enjoys singing and has a good voice
___ Can tell when a musical note is off-key

___ Has a good sense of rhythm
___ Can play an instrument "by ear"
___ Is able to keep time to music
___ Actively cares for a pet
___ Is attuned to the natural environment
___ Shows interest in weather and weather patterns
___ Enjoys working with plants and animals

___ Works effectively in a group
___ Is involved with clubs or groups
___ Takes on leadership roles
___ Enjoys being with people
___ Has good friendships
___ Identifies with and is sensitive to the feelings and moods of others
___ Picks up on verbal and non-verbal communication

___ Enjoys being alone
___ Is aware of own strengths and weaknesses
___ Keeps a journal or diary
___ Is reflective about self and the learning process
___ Can regulate personal feelings and moods

___ Excels in jigsaw puzzles, mazes, and visual puzzles
___ Draws accurately and well
___ Chooses to think and/or represent ideas in pictures
___ Can visualize how things would appear from a different point of view (i.e. bird's eye view)
___ Excels in geometry
___ Accurately reads and interprets maps, charts, and diagrams
___ Enjoys constructing models
___ Is sensitive to and aware of color and scenery
___ Is artistic

Figure 2–4 *Sample Student Profile [adapted from Armstrong (1992) and Haggerty (1995)]*

Miguel and his students, become evidence of what each individual values. As he explains:

> I keep a portfolio of the child's writing and other things she or he makes in a folder. This to me is the data on a child. I look at the piece of work when the child is making it. I listen to what the child says about this work. I try to make a note on the back of the paper of what they tell me. I also ask them if they think this piece of work is something they want to save for their portfolio. We decide together which pieces to save. Usually we choose memorable pieces that show lots of growth and competence.

Miguel's students collect their work in folders, then periodically select work as evidence of a growth area. Working on portfolio collection, selection, and reflection is a regular part of the weekly routine in Miguel's classroom.

Miguel sets aside thirty-five minutes after lunch on Fridays as his whole-class portfolio time. Every Friday, each student looks back through their folder at the weekly collection of work, making sure that each piece is dated. They select two or three pieces that show growth for that week, and write reflections on these pieces. These weekly selections and corresponding reflections are stapled, tagged, and saved in another folder (portfolio entries). While students are writing reflections on their work, Miguel conferences with two or three students who he has scheduled to meet with on that day. He keeps a calendar posted so students can sign up for monthly portfolio conferences.

Students know when they will regularly share their work with their teacher. Miguel has built a system into his daily routine so that he can sit beside as many children as possible each day. This is how he and other teachers make portfolios a part of their daily routine. The three key steps they follow in the portfolio process are: 1) collection of work, 2) selection of specific work that demonstrates growth, and 3) reflection on what the work represents.

To teach students how to reflect on their work, Miguel uses

four key reflection questions to help his students regularly take stock of their learning. He repeats these questions orally in class and they are posted in writing on the wall of his room.

As Miguel confesses:

> Yes, some families talk to their children and reflect on what they do, but I find that most children need to be taught how to reflect on what they do. In my experience children need to be given language for how to express their reflections in writing. We practice writing reflections during group meeting time and I create a chart of key vocabulary words and phrases to help them explain what they did and how they did it.

To facilitate the collection, selection, and reflection process, Miguel prepares weekly reflection sheets, which are attached to portfolio selections. Students look back at the piece they selected and then fill in their responses to the key reflection questions, noted in Figure 2–5.

For students who struggle to write, Miguel has them tape-record their reflections or he asks a volunteer or older student to help record what students say on the reflection sheet. This simple modification of the reflection process is useful for indi-

---

Portfolio Reflection Time

1. What did you do in this piece of work?

2. How did you do it? What materials did you use?

3. What did you learn by doing this piece of work?

Figure 2–5: *Portfolio Reflection Time*

viduals who are English language learners or have disabilities that make written expression a challenge. The student portfolio is one part of the documentation that Miguel shares with parents and other teachers about his students. His recorded observations of children, and the notes on their daily activities, add to this assessment collection. This collected data helps him compile his students' multiple intelligences profiles.

At the end of the year, his students compile approximately ten to twelve work samples that they have selected and reflected on to represent the entire school year's progress. This collection of student work representing all content areas is called the *pass-along portfolio*, which denotes the three-stage process—collection, selection, and reflection (see Figure 2–6).

Pass Along Portfolios

This end-of-year final portfolio—the *pass-along portfolio*—is evidence of growth over the school year. The portfolio contains student work samples from September, November, March, and June. The pass-along portfolio will be sent along to next year's teacher or to parents as evidence of each learner's accomplishments. At some schools, these portfolios are saved in a storage area or archive of student work. Mai-Mai's portfolio, as a pass-along portfolio, is an example of her first- and second-grade years' story as chronicled in ten pieces of work *(as shown on the CD).*

> It seems like I have to keep observing, documenting and keeping track of what they do, then I can constantly push them to do challenging work at the time when it is most possible (Miguel Guiterrez).

Designing an Interactive Environment: Spaces for Observing and Keeping Track

Miguel's classroom space and organization reflect his philosophy of teaching and learning as a sociocultural process based on

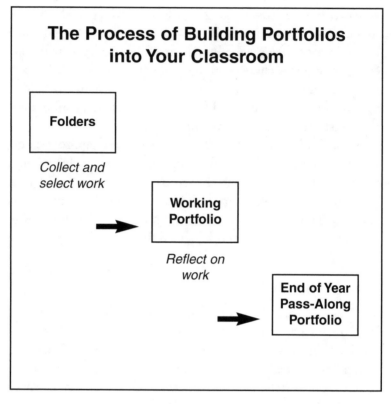

Figure 2–6: *The Process of Building Portfolios into Your Classroom*

interaction. Since his goal is to create a community of learners, he believes that the spaces that children occupy allow for work in small groups in which individual possessions and boundaries do not curtail their interactions. As Miguel explains:

> I want to create a community in this room and a sense that the work we do is done together. I am trying to design this into the physical space in the classroom.

> When each child has a separate desk, he or she cannot help but worry about their own property instead of shared property. If I had my choice, I would have no desks, and use tables and chairs, adult chairs, too, so they can feel big.

My observations in this classroom suggest that the physical environment helps create a setting in which Miguel can observe and interact frequently with each child, allowing him to create an MI profile of each individual. In his classroom, individual and group work takes place in smaller sectioned areas. There are strategically placed teacher observation chairs where Miguel can observe a single child and keep track of six others. Both he and his reading assistant become strategic observers and informal assessors of children as an integral part of their daily.

Each morning, Miguel rotates around the desks as part of his process of checking in on each child's reading and journal writing. His morning schedule every day begins with forty-five minutes of journal writing and drawing. After journal time, he has students write answers to open-ended questions that he draws from ideas expressed in student journals. These classroom conversations, built into independent writing time, allows Miguel "to size up" each child's daily written work. When he stops to look at student work, Miguel questions students about the piece they are working on.

These student-teacher interactions allow time for personalized or differentiated teaching where, as Miguel suggests, he identifies what he needs to teach to improve their writing. In essence, he is scaffolding the children's learning process by constantly asking questions, asking for revisions, and observing their responses:

> As I watch six children doing journals, I see they are confused about the words *there, their,* and *they're*. I stopped the whole group and asked them to tell me when each of these words is used. Then I do a mini-lesson on the board.

> They edit their journals and promise me that they understand this now. I ask them in their work to show me they understand specific spellings, meanings, and usage of the words *their, there,* and *they're*.

Miguel has developed a system for observing, keeping track, and documenting the work of his students that is built into his daily schedule and routine. Using the theory of multiple intelligences, Miguel does specific thinking and planning about the physical space of his classroom. Centers, he suggests, are built into the classroom to combine at least two or three intelligences—offering activities with multiple formats of expression—in words, in pictures, in art, in graphic format, in charts, or in audiotapes. As a reflective tool, Miguel uses a checklist to track his efforts to apply multiple intelligences, as illustrated in Figure 2–7.

Miguel's classroom includes observation areas and centers designed so that he can actively assess students by sitting beside them. He uses his classroom assessments to offer his students personalized opportunities for learning, and helping him plan MI-based activities. As he plans activities for his learners, he finds that creating focused activities that draw on linguistic or logical-mathematical intelligences is simple, but incorporating music, art, and exploration of nature is more difficult. In his classroom design, Miguel strategically works to include all the intelligences, which are often represented more concretely in specific activity areas:

- **Linguistic, Interpersonal, and Visual-Spatial**—Demonstrated in group meetings, shared reading areas
- **Logical-Mathematical, Interpersonal, and Bodily-Kinesthetic**—Demonstrated in games, math manipulatives
- **Musical and Bodily-Kinesthetic**—Demonstrated in group meetings, cassette area, and literacy chants
- **Visual-Spatial, Bodily-Kinesthetic, and Interpersonal**—Demonstrated in art center, LEGO area
- **Naturalistic, Interpersonal, and Bodily-Kinesthetic**—Demonstrated in group meetings, science center

Multiple Intelligences **Reflections on how they are used in my classroom**	**Examples of how I target intelligence Area(s)**	**Areas where I can emphasize this intelligence more**	**Ideas for portfolio implementation**
Logical/Mathematical			
Visual/Spatial			
Bodily/Kinesthetic			
Musical/Rhythmic			
Interpersonal/Reflection			
Interpersonal/Social			
Naturalistic/Nature			

Figure 2–7: *Reflections on Using Activities Based on MI Theory*

Miguel is constantly observing children and their prefer-ences in the classroom. For Miguel, the portfolio system and the physical layout of the classroom invite both teacher and learners to use MI theory to reflect on their personal learning experience during daily instruction.

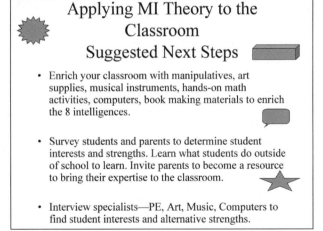

Figure 2–8: *Applying MI Theory to the Classroom—Suggested Next Steps*

Suggested Next Steps

- Provide students with self directed learning opportunities and independent project work so they can pursue interests in areas of study.

- Try to add activities that involve movement, music, visual arts, cooperative learning and self reflection.

- Use strengths as a bridge to weaknesses. If a student is strong mechanically and challenged linguistically, ask her to write a book explaining how to put together a clock.

Figure 2–9: *Suggested Next Steps*

Chapter 3

Multiple Intelligences and Portfolios: Creating a Learning Culture in a Classroom

EVANGELINE HARRIS STEFANAKIS WITH
KATHLEEN GUINEE

MI and portfolio assessment started to make sense to me when I came to work at the Cambridgeport School, which as a whole school, is designed around a belief in multiple intelligences and multiple assessments.

(Bela Bhasin)

*H*ow do teachers as classroom leaders, and principals as school leaders each contribute to creating a portfolio culture? The teacher stories in Chapters 3 through 6 describe the work of Bela (grades 1/2), Sarah (grades 5/6), and Jill (grades 7/8); and they portray the developmental stories of portfolio work of accomplished teachers across a K through 8 continuum. The next two chapters describe poignant stories of an early childhood teacher, Bela Bhasin, and her principal, Lynn F. Stuart, who explain how a portfolio culture has been created in a classroom and in a whole-school community.

Clarity of vision and purpose, placing children at the center of the assessment conversation, is apparent in Lynn Stuart's description in the next chapter of a whole-school portfolio culture. Her overview of the Cambridgeport School's evolution, in assessment reform provides a context for understanding how portfolios adapt to the setting they represent. Lynn's leadership story provides the essential framework for seeing how multiple intelligences (MI) and portfolios can create a learning culture in a school. It also provides a strong background for looking at the different approaches of teachers in grades 4 through 8, each of whom have to accommodate different students' developmental stages.

Additionally, each of these next three chapters present a gallery of portfolios (representing students from grades 1–8), with teacher-developed resources and materials included on the accompanying CD. Each of the students whose portfolio entries you see and hear about on the CD provide multiple intelligences profiles of individual learners. The material to create portfolio gallery begins to offer evidence of how to best assess and teach all students, including those who are bilingual or have special education needs.

A Portrait: Creating a Portfolio System in Bela's Grade 1/2 Classroom

Like Miguel in Chapter 2, Bela Bhasin, a primary teacher at the Cambridgeport School, uses a portfolio system as a window into her learners' minds, looking and listening to her students and what they can do. In her classroom, Bela uses portfolios to help develop individual profiles of students based on the theory of multiple intelligences. Teaching students in her grades 1 and 2 multi-age classroom, Bela has been refining her portfolio culture for the past seven years. She describes how MI theory and portfolios define many of her classroom practices:

> Over the years I strengthened my understanding of multiple intelligences by reading and by observing children. As a theory it helped me look into the academic work that my students do to better understand their strengths and weaknesses. Portfolios have helped me see that all children have intelligences in different areas. Carefully looking at their work has helped me see where their strengths are.

Bela creates a multiple intelligences profile of her students while she examines work from their portfolios.

I find that using collections of 8 to 10 pieces of work has helped me each child's multiple intelligences. In Mai-Mai's portfolio, what strikes me is how much writing is an important part of who she is and how she expresses herself. Looking at her portfolio you can see that more writing shows up, in art, in math, in social studies, than you see in other children's collections. Then I look at her writing, her art, and her math pieces—you see how much attention she pays to details, which are very important to her. Those are the kind of things it is hard to miss when you use portfolios. She has very strong linguistic and visual-spatial skills for her age, but other areas need to be developed.

As Bela looks at collections of student work, she notes where each child has areas of strength so she can better tailor her teaching to build on them.

Mai-Mai's and Xavy's portfolios show they have very different profiles as learners even though each of them, at times, struggled in writing areas.

We could see in their work collections that coming from bilingual and bicultural backgrounds they showed highly developed skills in telling stories through their drawings and project work.

They each had different areas of challenge. Mai-Mai, who came to the U.S. at 3 when she was adopted from China, was showing so much of her daily language development. Through her art and math work samples, she showed me she understood the languages involved with learning in these subjects.

Xavy, who spoke two different languages to each of his parents, used art and project work to help express his ideas initially. Writing down ideas took longer for Xavy. We could help him learn language as he selected and reflected on a collection of pieces for his portfolio. Xavy needed help in oral language to grow in written language.

Mai-Mai and Xavy's portfolio samples are on the CD-ROM.

In Bela's words, portfolios are great equalizers. They speak to an individual child's strengths rather than to what they do not know. As she watches student reactions, she knows that portfolios are powerful assessment tools, which have special meaning for the children who create them.

> Of all the assessments that I have tried with students, portfolios are the ones that never fail. There is a look of pride that I see on students' faces as they make their first portfolio. They have that portfolio in their hands showing pieces that show their growth from September to December, then to June.

> Even if the student has trouble throughout the year, he or she has put enough work into that portfolio just like every other child in the room. To document this, I took pictures on portfolio day of students walking in. They were holding their portfolios so close to them. Right from the cover, which is their self-portrait, to what goes inside—it's all theirs.

Bela believes that because portfolios reflect students' multiple intelligences, they are equally effective for all kinds of students, including those with bilingual or special educational needs. In an interview, I asked Bela to describe how she manages her portfolio system, specifically how her students collect, select, and reflect on their work. As she reminded me, creating a workable portfolio system takes time, about three years. So she recommended starting slow and small, beginning with just collecting work. To understand her portfolio system, Bela suggests looking first at her daily classroom practices to see how portfolios capture students' daily work.

What does a typical day in Bela's classroom entail? How does she apply the MI theory in teaching and assessing her students? How is assessment a daily learning experience that is built into the instructional program? What does Bela's classroom look like and how does that help her manage the portfolio assessment process?

A Portrait of Bela's Portfolio Classroom—
A Typical Day (with Kathleen Guinee)*

Even before entering Bela's grade 1/2classroom, the importance of and respect for student work is obvious. The walls of the stairwell leading up to the classroom are lined with student work. On the landing is an autumnal mural of a park with colored leaves on the trees and ground. Poems describing how leaves look, feel, move, and sound are arranged above the painting. Along the wall of the upper half of the staircase are poems and tissue paper pictures about Cambridge. Both sides of the doorframe into Bela's room are covered with student drawings.

Entering the room, an observer is awed by the student work, its quantity and its content. The back of Bela's crowded desk is to the left of the entrance and a computer and printer are on a rectangular table on the right (see classroom diagram, Figure 3–1). This half of the classroom contains three hexagonal tables. A rectangular table runs perpendicular to the front of the teacher's desk. Many of the items in the room, including the tables and the chairs around them, are labeled with colored tags naming the objects in Spanish. A brown rug, on which little pieces of masking tape mark a semicircle of student's names, dominates the other half of the classroom. Student artwork fills the walls of the room.

The student work around the room reflects the multiple intelligences theory implemented in the classroom. One project on display involves the visual-spatial, linguistic, and intrapersonal intelligences. It consists of construction paper with a student-drawn and colored self-portrait on one half and sentence stems in the format "As _____ as a _____" on the other half. Nancy, with blonde hair, blue eyes, and a turquoise shirt, describes herself as being "as lovele as a ros in a girdn." Maurice, a dark-skinned, dark-haired boy with a red shirt,

---

*This excerpt is adapted from a paper written by Kathleen Guinee, research assistant and doctoral candidate at Harvard Graduate School of Education, in conjunction with the course work of T-160 Understanding Learning Challenges taught by Dr. Evangeline Harris Stefanakis (December 2000).

considers himself "as fast as an ant"; and Seth, a boy with brown hair, a gray shirt, and a peace-sign necklace, thinks he's "as tough as a tornado." Often a piece of student work that will later become part of a portfolio is also displayed in the room. Bela has students put sticky notes on displayed pieces that they want to put into their portfolios. Hanging above the class are construction paper booklets. On the front of each booklet, wrinkled paper surrounds a photo of a student. The covers are labeled with the titles "Who I Am" and "Who in the World Am I?" Later in the year, these booklets will become part of a collection documenting each student's growth during the school year.

Not all the work students complete in Bela's room is on display. Under the windows near the hexagonal tables are four work crates labeled math folders, language arts folders, science folders, and unfinished work folders. Each crate contains a set of brightly colored folders. As students complete their written work, they move it from their unfinished work folder to the appropriate subject area folder. A bench running perpendicular to these crates contains the yellow Writing Workshop folders in four bins labeled Planning, Writing, Editing, and Publishing.

In addition to influencing the student work around the room, multiple intelligences theory is present in other decorations. For instance, the corner of the room diagonal to the door could be considered the nature corner, reflecting visual-spatial and the naturalistic intelligence. It is home to a fish tank and several types of plants, large and small, as well as posters about trees and leaves. Multiple intelligences also influences teacher and student behavior in the classroom. Specifically, one strategy for quieting the class and getting the students' attention uses the interpersonal and the musical intelligence focusing on rhythms. The teacher claps in rhythm, and then the class claps the rhythm back.

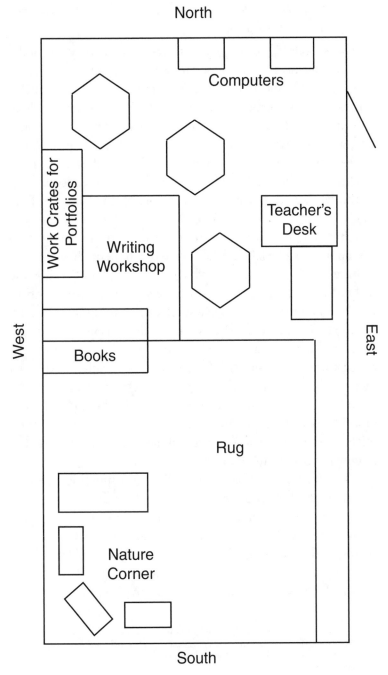

Figure 3–1: *Diagram of Bela's Classroom*

Morning Meeting Time: Group Learning Based on Multiple Intelligences (with Kathleen Guinee)

Meeting sounds like an activity that would require only two of the eight intelligences, linguistic and interpersonal, but in Bela's classroom, the daily morning meeting encompasses all eight intelligences. The students sit in assigned spots forming a large semicircle on the rug. The semicircle opens toward the south wall, which contains a bulletin board holding the day-of-the-week display, the days-in-school counter, and the monthly calendar.

During meeting time, the Meeting Leader spreads the day-of-the-week cards on the rug, and then asks the Calendar Person, "Today is . . . ?" The Calendar Person selects the matching day-of-the-week card, turns around, and hangs it on the appropriately labeled hook on the bulletin board. This routine continues for "Yesterday was . . . .?" and "Tomorrow will be . . . .?" then repeats with the Calendar Person identifying the same three days of the week in Spanish. One day during the meeting, when asked what the day was in Spanish, the Calendar Person said, "Help." Students in the semicircle raised their hands and the Calendar Person called on one to receive a hint about which card to select. After selecting the six day-of-the-week cards, the Calendar Person moves to the monthly calendar to identify the number of the date, and then selects and decorates a construction paper square to put on the calendar, marking the date.

After finishing the day-of-the-week and monthly calendar activities, the Recorder changes the counter that records how many days the students have been in school this year. This counter consists of cards with digits and pouches with straws corresponding to the hundreds, tens, and ones places. After changing the digits and straws, the Recorder identifies which digit is the tens place and which is the ones place.

---

*This excerpt is adapted from a paper written by Kathleen Guinee, research assistant and doctoral candidate at Harvard Graduate School of Education, in conjunction with the course work of T-160 Understanding Learning Challenges taught by Dr. Evangeline Harris Stefanakis (December 2000).

Next, the students raise their hands to volunteer to read the date and different colored sentences the teacher wrote on a whiteboard easel. The Meeting Leader selects students to read each sentence and follows the text with a pointer as they read. The teacher encourages students who have not yet participated in the meeting to raise their hands to read. The first sentence is a greeting in a foreign language, such as Greek or French. The other sentences are about the weather and what the class is going to do that day. Through these sentences, Bela incorporates the linguistic, naturalistic, and sometimes intrapersonal intelligences into meeting time. For instance, one morning the weather sentence was about the rainstorm of the day before. Bela asked the students if they knew how many inches of snow would have fallen if all the rain from the day before had been snow. As the students guessed the number of inches, Bela gave them hints by saying that the answer was greater or less than a previous guess.

Thus, Bela narrows the possibilities until the students guess the correct number of inches. As an example of a sentence that incorporated the linguistic and intrapersonal intelligence one Monday morning, the board read, "Did you have a good weekend?" After one student read the question, other students raised their hands to tell the class whether they had a good or a bad weekend and why.

After the students read the sentences, Bela erases the whiteboard and writes the number of days the students have been in school. She then asks the students what other numbers they can make with those digits. After all the numbers have been named and written on the board, a student draws sticks representing each item in the tens place and dots representing each item in the ones place for each number. Then, the teacher asks the class which number is largest and why. This activity further incorporates the logical-mathematical and visual-spatial intelligences into meeting time. After integrating the musical and bodily-kinesthetic intelligences, the meeting concludes with Flavia, the assistant teacher, leading the students in song.

Many of the songs have hand motions to go along with the lyrics to engage the learners in these favorite activities.

Activities in Bela's Class: Writing and Math Creates Student Work*

Meeting is not the only activity in Bela's class that incorporates multiple intelligences theory in both curricular and assessment activities. For instance, every student in the class keeps a journal, which uses the linguistic, visual-spatial, and intrapersonal intelligences. The journals are bright orange folders that contain pages with a lined section for writing and a blank area for drawing, a half page for each in the first-grade journals, and a full page in the second-grade journals. The students record stories, both true and fictional, and draw illustrative pictures in these journals.

For example, one morning Nancy wrote a story about finding a twelve-point snowflake in wintertime. She then drew a picture of the snowflake. Another student wrote about waking up in the morning in her striped pajamas and going to her guinea pig's cage to tell him she loved him. Journal writing incorporates linguistic and the interpersonal intelligence. The students share their stories and drawings with one another and ask for help with spelling. In addition, I observed a second-grade student help a first-grade student with the general journal writing procedures, explaining to her how to draw an arrow at the bottom of a page to indicate that the story would continue on the next page.

Math activities in Bela's class also involve the use of multiple intelligences. For example, one day the second graders exercised their logical-mathematical, bodily-kinesthetic, and interpersonal intelligences while completing a worksheet involving calculators. Each student wrote four to six addition and subtraction problems to solve with a calculator. After solv-

---

*This excerpt is adapted from a paper written by Kathleen Guinee, research assistant and doctoral candidate at Harvard Graduate School of Education, in conjunction with the course work of T-160 Understanding Learning Challenges taught by Dr. Evangeline Harris Stefanakis (December 2000).

Activities During Meeting That Combine Different Intelligences

Intelligences to Observe	Classroom Activity
Linguistic-Interpersonal/ Logical-Mathematical	Today, tomorrow, and yesterday day-of-the-week cards in English and Spanish Colored sentences on whiteboard
Logical-Mathematical/Visual-Spatial	Days in school using straw counters What other numbers can be made with these digits?
Naturalistic/Linguistic	Whiteboard sentence about weather
Visual-Spatial/Bodily-Kinesthetic	Calendar person selects color and decorates calendar square Pouches of straws representing ones and tens places of days in school Dots and lines to represent tens and ones places of "what other numbers can be made"
Musical/Interpersonal	Meeting concludes with a song
Bodily-Kinesthetic/Interpersonal/ Logical-Mathematical	Song uses hand and body motions Calendar Person selects day-of-the-week cards and hangs them on hooks Recorder of Days in School changes digits and straws for days in school
Interpersonal/Intrapersonal	Whole Class Activity Student leading meeting chooses students to read sentences Whiteboard question asks students if they had a good weekend

Created by Evangeline Harris Stefanakis and Kathleen Guinee

ing their own problems, the students traded papers to verify their calculations. The students marked any discrepancies with a question mark (?) and developed a strategy to resolve the discrepancies together.

Another morning, the first graders applied their logical-mathematical, bodily-kinesthetic, and visual-spatial intelligences to a math activity. Each student had a ten-unit-long rod, a portion of which was one color and the remainder another. The students colored strips of paper to match the rod and then glued the strips to their worksheet.

How does a program like Bela's, which incorporates the multiple intelligences in its curriculum, integrate a portfolio system? How does a teacher like Bela think, plan, and organize a portfolio-assessment system that she can manage allowing students to do a major part of the work? In a series of interviews after school, Bela outlined her key practices for thinking, planning, and effectively working with portfolios in the early grades.

Bela's Portfolio System: A Collection of Strategies for Thinking and Planning

Over time, Bela has developed strategies that make portfolios less work for the teacher and more of a daily classroom routine that students can work on by themselves. This is the only way, according to Bela, that this can work when she has twenty-five students in the classroom. She has identified some key classroom practices that help her use portfolios to know her children and know how to best teach them. Overall, Bela has identified six strategies for managing portfolios with a large group.

1. Start with an Area in the Room—A Place to Sit Beside Students to Guide Collection of Work Samples

In Bela's classroom, students have a place and procedure for collecting work:

> I've always had an area in the room where there are folders and places where children's work is collected, stamped with the date,

and displayed. We start the year just by keeping work in a folder. As time goes on, I've tried to guide students in terms of what pieces they should select and keep for their portfolios.

For example, some students want to show off their writing and then select a handwriting piece, so we discuss it. Your handwriting, I tell them, can also be seen through your stories and that also shows who you are as a writer.

So, giving students guidance about how to select pieces that show several skills at once helps them make choices for their portfolios. What they select is a clue to me of what is important to that individual student and a clue to me about their multiple intelligences.

2. Create Portfolios Representing All Curricular Areas—Use a Selection Checklist

Bela has created a format for having students themselves select works that are prime pieces for their portfolio collection (see Figure 3–2). She outlines her format for broadening the selection of student work using a selection checklist:

Students are capable of looking through their folders and selecting work that shows growth. So I started using a selection checklist sheet for students to do the portfolio selections themselves. The checklist sheet is divided into the subject areas: writing, reading, math, science, and social studies, and students can select 3 pieces for each subject.

Each student sits down with his or her folder to look back over work samples. They put a mark on three pieces that they want to choose for writing and they fill that in on their sheet. Then they look for three reading pieces, three math pieces, and so forth. They fill out the portfolio selection form and bring it to me. I look it over, and then they're ready to go on to do their reflections. There is some teaching of the selection process involved to get this started.

Bela's selection checklist is a way to broaden the collection and help students add work that demonstrates a range of skills in a subject area. In many ways the checklist helps Bela as she tries to create an MI profile, ensuring that student work from many areas is represented. She asks her students to think about what evidence they have that they know a specific skill or idea.

Often the skills Bela has asked students to look for are aligned with the state learning standards and curriculum frameworks. In mathematics or in other subjects, she models in class meetings how to make selections according to learning standards.

> With a subject like math, because we do a great deal of practice on operations and story problems, we had too many pieces to select from. What I did was to help students learn how to make selections that show different math skill areas we have been learning.

> During a class meeting time, I demonstrated how to vary math portfolio selections by picking one piece that's from our addition or subtraction work, one piece that showed some data collection, one piece that showed number sentences, etc. After that, I watched the children go through their work and suggest, "Let's see, for data collection I want this one." That was beneficial for a lot of students because it helped them focus on finding evidence of different skills in each piece they selected.

> *Samples of three students' portfolios from Bela's classroom are on the CD-ROM.*

3. Create Weekly Practice for Writing Reflections—Use Learning Logs to Guide the Process

Reflection is part of our daily practice from the beginning of school and it is something, in fact, I struggle with. I'm not sure how developmentally appropriate it is for first graders to do a reflection sheet. For me, it's a very important skill for them to talk about and then to write about. Bela uses a weekly learning log that students do to help them reflect on what they did and what they learned. For each day, Monday to Friday, students think about what they worked on and comment in their learning log—talking and reflecting on specific work they select to write about (as shown in Figure 3–3).

Portfolio Planner

Name_____

Writing

What did you choose?	Date	Reflection	Arranged
1.			
2.			
3.			

Math

What did you choose?	Date	Reflection	Arranged
1.			
2.			
3.			

Reading

What did you choose?	Date	Reflection	Arranged
1.			
2.			
3.			

Social Studies and Science

What did you choose?	Date	Reflection	Arranged
1.			
2.			
3.			

Art or anything else

What did you choose?	Date	Reflection	Arranged
1.			
2.			

Are these finished? ☐ self-portrait   ☐ All About You page

Figure 3–2: *Portfolio Planner (adapted from Bela Bhasin's design)*

4. Develop Systematic Monthly Reflection and Goal-Setting by Using a Monthly Review

At the end of the month we continue to set specific learning goals as individuals. I have students do a monthly review reflection sheet (see Figure 3–4) using four questions that I developed for each developmental level. Students in grades 1 and 2 start off with the same questions:

Weekly Work Record

Monday: _ _ _ _ _ _ _ _ _ _ _ _ _ _ _ _ _ _

One thing that I worked on today was: _____

My response: _____

_____

- -

Tuesday: _ _ _ _ _ _ _ _ _ _ _ _ _ _ _ _ _

One thing that I worked on today was: _____

My response: _____

_____

- -

Wednesday: _ _ _ _ _ _ _ _ _ _ _ _ _ _ _ _ _

One thing that I worked on today was: _____

My response: _____

_____

- -

Thursday: _ _ _ _ _ _ _ _ _ _ _ _ _ _ _ _ _

One thing that I worked on today was: _____

My response: _____

_____

- -

Friday: _ _ _ _ _ _ _ _ _ _ _ _ _ _ _ _ _

One thing that I worked on today was: _____

My response: _____

_____

Figure 3–3: *Weekly Work Record (adapted from Bela Bhasin's design)*

1. Think of a piece of work that you're most proud of. What do you like best about this piece?
2. Think of a piece of work that's been the most challenging. What made it challenging?

Then I vary what I do for younger and older students on question 3.

3. Grade 1: Draw a picture of an activity that you really enjoyed doing in school.

    Grade 2: Think of something you still need to work on. Why do you need to work on it?

The fourth question for both grades 1 and 2 students is:

4. Choose one piece of work to put in your portfolio and tell why you chose that piece.

5. Work on Display in the Classroom Is Tagged for the Portfolio Collection

Often the student work is on display in the room and we know that at a later date that piece is one we want to keep in our portfolio. I give my students a little sticker and they put it on that piece of work (a special tag). When I take the work down I know that it's supposed to go in the portfolio collection rather than their regular folders of work.

Photos that display the student work in Bela's classroom are on the CD-ROM.

6. Continue to Set Goals for Collecting, Selecting, and Reflecting on Student Work

The choice for the year-end, or pass-along portfolio still happens at the end of the year when we have to select only ten pieces as that year's story. What happens is they're choosing only one piece every month. So I don't always get a representation of all the different curriculum areas each month. After first grade it's easier since the idea of selecting work and the idea of a portfolio is not new to them. My goal for them by the time they leave me in grade 2 is that they become familiar with setting goals, selecting work, and thinking about why they want that piece of work in their

Monthly Review

Which piece of work are you most proud of? What do you like best about this piece of work?

_____

_____

_____

_____

Which piece of work was most challenging for you? What made it challenging?

_____

_____

_____

_____

Draw (and label) a picture of an activity you enjoyed doing this month.

Which piece of work did you choose to put in your portfolio? Why did you choose this piece?

_____

_____

_____

Figure 3–4: *Monthly Review (adapted from Bela Bhasin's design)*

portfolio. Eventually, through the learning log and monthly review, reflection as a process becomes clearer to them.

If we look at the pass-along portfolio from Bela's classroom, we can see how this process of collection, selection, and reflection works. *Examine grade 1 and 2 work samples on the CD-ROM.*

Bela's portfolio system explicitly teaches a process for reflection that has many parts involving talking, reading, and writing. Despite a great deal of practice she finds that young children cannot easily reflect on their work. As she reminds us:

> It seems that some students reflect more because they are asked to do this at home. In our classroom community, we help others develop a language to use in reflection—not just to write, "I chose it because I like it," but to think, "Tell about one thing that you like about your piece of work and say why you like it."

The challenge of reflection in primary-age children is apparent as we look at Mai-Mai's first-grade portfolio. In a reflection in September, Mai-Mai demonstrated how this still was not her process:

- What did you choose to put in your portfolio? Mai-Mai answers: "A reading tape."
- Why did you choose this piece? "Bela and Roseann asked me to put it in."
- What does this show about your learning? "It shows people want to hear someone reading."

By January, her reflections are more elaborate, "I chose this because I knew it showed when I drew my best flowers," indicating how she now sees her own growth.

In Xavy's and Mai-Mai's portfolios the growth in self-awareness as well as linguistic and intrapersonal intelligence is evident in the length and quality of their written reflections, (comparing September's work with May's work).

Samples of Xavy's and Mai-Mai's reflections which note the changes from September to May are on the CD-ROM.

Assessment as a Learning Experience—A Summary

Through collecting, selecting, and reflecting on student work, as Miguel, and Bela describe, young learners take ownership of their learning. They learn to select and reflect on their work, eventually becoming more independent of the teacher, as Bela outlines in her classroom portfolio system. Looking at student work present in Mai-Mai's, Xavy's, and Kenny's portfolios, Bela makes educational decisions fromcollections of her students' work. Portfolios help her know what to teach and how to teach specific content to her diverse learners. Portfolios, as collections of student work, are a vital means for all individuals, teachers, and students to look back and take stock of what they know and what they need to know. In essence, portfolios as data offer the teacher and the learner a way to capture the social and intellectual interaction of their learning—to see their growth—to mutually set goals for their improvement.

In the next chapter, Lynn F. Stuart, Bela's principal, tells her story of creating a whole-school culture, not only a classroom culture, built around portfolios. She reminds us to begin by looking at how both students and teachers learn and grow.

Chapter 4

Multiple Intelligences and Portfolios: Creating a Learning Culture in a Whole-School Setting

LYNN F. STUART

When I was in preschool, I wasn't very smart but every year I am at the Cambridgeport School, I get smarter and smarter.

(Jason, seventh-grade student)

A thirteen-year-old captures the essence of what all schools try to be—places where smartness grows. Yet all too often, being smart in school is the domain of the few, and abandoned as a goal by others who cannot find their way in places where *smart* is defined as a singular and static quality. Either you have it or you don't. But Jason understood something deeper. Being smart is multifaceted. Being smart isn't fixed. Getting smarter is at the heart of the matter. Communicating smartness occurs in rich and varied ways.

Let's look more closely at Jason's elementary school career. A Haitian-American student who came from a large family, Jason lives in a small apartment with older siblings who help their mother to support the family. His family did not frequently participate in the life of the school—they had other important tasks. In an interview conducted by first- and second-grade students who were studying the theme of community, Jason remembered back to his Head Start days and noted that he wasn't very smart.

Indeed, his portfolio shows how limited his experiences and his language were in his early childhood years, how he grew to master the English language in new and powerful ways, and how he also became one of the strongest leaders among all our students as he matured. Jason was a friend to all; he was a peacemaker in conflict; he was mischievous and adventurous; he was a confident learner.

In June 2000, at his eighth-grade portfolio presentation before a panel of community members, administrators, and teachers, his family proudly joined him to watch him describe his four portfolio projects and respond to questions from the panel. His confidence and competence were apparent to all present. Jason's efforts all along the way played an important part in his growth and development. The context in which he was taught at school was also an important part of his learning. It was a whole-school effort, as it must be, to understand and support the family of learners within.

The stories of Bela's, Jill's, and Sarah's classrooms that Evangeline Stefanakis portrays in this book describe children and teachers at work in a school that has a common set of beliefs about learning and teaching. These beliefs are the foundation of a shared philosophy and ways of learning together. They wrap around each teacher, child, and family to create a sense of shared purpose and direction. The students whose portfolio entries and voices you hear in this book present a unique profile of individual learners. Similarly, the chapters that describe Bela, Jill, and Sarah capture the qualities of accomplished teachers. What is vitally important is that they operate in the context of a whole school on a mission to create a better community in which learning prospers for all members, whether they be children or adults.

The First Step: Developing Shared Beliefs About Learning and Teaching

The first imperative for good schools, it seems to me, is to understand learning. The need to understand teaching follows, for as Don Holdaway (1983) so cogently reminded us, it is important to put the "learning horse before the teaching cart." Multiple intelligences (MI) theory has provided important insights into the varied and unique ways that individuals learn and communicate. The foundational base for understanding how learning occurs has been described (Holdaway 1983) as natural, social learning. Learning begins with powerful models and immersion in an environment that values particular domains—reading, solving mathematical problems, dancing, drawing, bicycle riding, exploring the natural world, and so on.

The learner then joins the skillful model by participating alongside. This participation is often clumsy, approximating the skill in early forms. The third step in learning occurs as learners role-play or practice the skill in self-regulating ways with the skilled models available to assist, knowing when to teach, encourage, and affirm progress. Finally, the learner per- forms for self and a larger audience as the skill becomes more and more accomplished. Developmental learning theory has deepened our understanding that learning occurs over time. Across cultures, there is remarkably broad consistency in the developmental stages from childhood to adulthood. Most tasks' degree of difficulty is enhanced by both age and practice over time. We know, however, that learning is also grounded in culture—that is, the belief systems of family and the larger culture that surrounds an individual. Each one of these ways of understanding learning leads us to the importance of real- world contexts, the importance of meaning-making, and to the importance of the individual in relation to other learners and teachers. Learning does not occur in isolation, although prac- tice may take place in solitude. Learning is fundamentally social and interactional.

This broad view of learning leads directly to the questions of how to teach. First, we must understand the learner. Then, we must focus on the models, the instruction, and the conditions that allow for sustained practice of skills in context. Deep understanding of what we teach is also a prerequisite. We can- not teach what we do not know thoroughly. Instruction is the art of demonstrating what we know in engaging ways. Teaching and learning are fundamentally acts of engagement.

The goal of understanding learning is always before us at the Cambridgeport School. As we ask ourselves questions of how children learn and how we can teach effectively and differently so that each may learn, we are drawn to the compelling need to make learning visible. We have come to believe that *observation* of learning and the collection of student work are fundamental to the cycle of learning, teaching, and assessment. Portfolios of student work and reflections offer a window into the learner, the learning, and the teaching. The reflective process of seeking to understand learning and teaching has the power to generate new theory and new practice.

The Second Step: Creating a School Culture in Which Learning Can Prosper

The second condition for good schools is a culture of collaboration in a community. If a school is simply a collection of individual students and their individual teachers, it lacks the capabilities to reach high standards, no matter how committed and intelligent individual members are. The challenge becomes one of creating a whole-school environment in which all within the community learn to observe, understand and nurture learning in rich and multiple ways.

Much is written about individual teachers and their individual practices. However, much less is written about whole-school efforts to create a culture of learning. Judith Warren Little's pioneering work in the late 1970s and early 1980s illuminated the power of the collaborative work of teachers (Little 1982). Jon Saphier and Matthew King reminded us that "Good seeds grow in strong cultures" (Saphier and King 1985). A comprehensive research study at the University of Wisconsin (Newmann and Wehlege, 1995) clearly documented the importance of teacher collaboration in the learning of students.

A professional community and student performance are linked inextricably. It is this notion of a professional culture in a school that focuses our attention on what is possible for students and teachers. At the Cambridgeport School, we have always valued and deeply respected this truth about professional community. The varied ways in which our teachers work together is testament to the belief that the incredibly hard work of teaching diverse learners can really only be accomplished in a community. No one can go it alone. *(Chapter 7 describes in detail the ways in which the Cambridgeport School faculty works together.)*

The Cambridgeport School: A Place Where Learning and Community Are Central

The Cambridgeport School is a "young" public school that began in 1990 with one kindergarten class of twenty students. By 2001, the school has grown to sixteen classes and more than 300 students, kindergarten through grade 8. All classes beyond kindergarten are multigraded. The school population reflects the racial, ethnic, educational, and economic diversity of the city. Approximately 51% of the student body is comprised of students of color, 30% of students come from Afro-Aerican backgrounds, 10% Latino, 8% are of Asian background. Aporoximately 20% qualify for free *and* reduced lunch.

It is a school at which demographic differences and individual learning differences among students create both opportunity and challenge. Conceived from the beginning as a school that valued active, project-based curriculum; multiple ways of learning; and multiple ways of documenting learning, we began to build a culture in which all learn together. Purposefully small, because we wanted every adult and student to know every other adult and student, the school was structured as a place where teachers would work in grade-level teams and be a strong part of decision making. Families, too, have been instrumental in the life of the school from the very beginning, from work parties of painting and building furniture to volunteering in classrooms to participating in the governing board of the school, the School Council.

Demographic Characteristics of the Cambridgeport School, 2001	
Population: K–8	300 students
Male/Female Students	150/150
Racial/Ethnic Breakdown	American Indian (3 students), Black (92 students), Hispanic (31 students), Asian (24 students), White (150 students)
Free/Reduced Lunch	75 students
Faculty	Approximately 50 percent teachers of color, approximately 33 percent men

The school's first decade has been both arduous and exhilarating. Like all public schools, we have been challenged with the demands of a bureaucratic system that is struggling with big questions of accountability and organizational structures that often lack efficiency and attention to school-based needs. Standardized and state testing take significant amounts of time to administer, and threaten the delicate balance between broad snapshots of schools and rigorous and exciting learning of individual students in their classrooms. An outgrown rental building gave us a wonderful start, but we had to endure years of waiting for a permanent home. We are, in some ways, like every public school, struggling and expected to "produce" the workers for tomorrow's jobs. We refocused our efforts from a production line to a community that works together toward building productive lives full of interests, skills, and awareness of others. This has opened doors to learning for adults and students alike.

Clarifying the Purposes of Assessment

At a summer workshop and at many subsequent meetings, we visited and revisited the purposes of assessment. We believe that the fundamental purposes of assessment are to *improve student learning* and to *improve teaching*. Within these two broad categories, we have come to define essential qualities of assessment as shown in the following chart.

Purposes of Assessment

Improving Student Learning

- Making learning visible to students
- Fostering reflective learning which becomes increasingly self-regulating
- Acknowledging and celebrating learning
- Communicating learning to families and the wider community

Improving Teaching

- Adjusting instruction to meet the needs of individual students
- Fostering reflective teaching which informs practice
- Acknowledging and celebrating teaching
- Communicating learning to multiple constituencies
- Improving the capacity of schools to reach for high standards for student achievement

---

Documentation of Learning: Creating a Portfolio for Every Student

At the heart of our work is the belief that observation and documentation of students engaged in their work at school will guide teaching practice and professional growth. Thus, from the very beginning, the school maintained folders of student work. We called our collections of work *portfolios*. The truth was that we, like many others, were doing more collecting than anything else. We knew that we wanted to collect work over time and maintain an archive of each student's yearly work from kindergarten until eighth-grade graduation. Those early years were messy years, with a great deal of work collected through trial and error as we struggled with questions of purpose, use, and organization:

- How much can we actually save without being overrun with piles of student work?
- What is the role of the arts in student portfolios?
- How can we structure the entries to reflect the breadth and depth of student thinking in various intelligences?
- How can we organize student work more systematically?
- Do we include work in progress to show growth over time?
- What are the possibilities of electronic portfolios?
- How shall we use the portfolios?

As our questions and focus became clearer, we began to develop a Framework for K–8 Portfolios to guide our portfolio practices across the school (see Figure 4–1).

First Steps in Creating a Portfolio for Every Child

Armed with a sense of purpose, the next question is always, "Where do I begin?" Documentation of student learning is complicated and requires a sense of adventure and organization. There is adventure because you don't really know where the road will take you, and organization because only if you organize and reorganize along the way will it ever make sense. That is how we forged ahead. It is important to *just do it*, that is, to sit beside the learner whenever you can to document and collect. It is equally important to set a pace that does not overwhelm while you find an organizational style that works in your setting.

A School-Based System of Assessment with the Student and Teacher at the Center: High Standards and Accountability

As a school that has high standards for student learning and acknowledges the importance of multiple indicators of

Cambridgeport School
Cambridge, Massachusetts

A Framework for K–8 Portfolios

Introduction:

This portfolio framework has been developed by a representative faculty team focused on professional development and documentation. The dual purpose student portfolios are to show growth over time and represent the range of individual abilities. Portfolios are a celebration of student learning and strengths. Portfolios are shared periodically throughout the year with parents and members of the community at November and April conferences, and in June on Portfolio Day.

Preface:

This portfolio collection will be tied to the Massachusetts State Frameworks and Quarterly Assessments in the school. Work is selected both by teachers and students. Below is a general outline of portfolio contents for the whole-school community.

Portfolio Contents:

1. Cover has a portrait of the child for the year
2. A Table of Contents/Cover Letter
3. Language Arts—2–3 pieces from Beginning, Middle, End of the Year
   A. Reading—logs, audiotapes, retelling
   B. Writing—including rough drafts, revisions, products, and illustrations. *Possible examples include Narrative, Poetry, Letters, Expository Research, Journals, Science/Math Writing, Persuasive Writing*
   C. Oratory example
4. Math—2–3 pieces from Beginning, Middle, End of the Year
   A. Work in different categories—including worksheets, problem-based work
   B. Math—examples may include graphs, journals, operations, geometry, projects, problem solving, open-ended questions, computer projects
5. Social Studies—1–2 pieces from Fall and Spring
   Large projects or group work can be photographed
   Group process can be documented using learning logs
6. Science—1–2 pieces Fall and Spring from required units
   Large projects or group work can be photographed
   Work may be interdisciplinary and combine subject area study-themes
   Group process can be documented using learning logs
7. Arts and Music—1 piece
   One project can be photographed
   Audiotapes and videotapes of music performances
8. Special Areas—*Profile of the Individual Students and Who They Are*
   Electronic Music—Jazz Disc
   A section—the most important thing about me
   Individual stories, honors, birthdays, field trips, performances

Figure 4-1: *A Framework for K-8 Portfolios*

First Steps in Creating

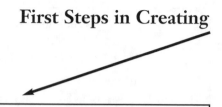

The teacher starts...

1. **Start small, go slowly.**
    * Save work in all subject areas and themes or units.
    * Find a place to keep work, organize it to meet your needs.
    * Talk with students about their work.
    * Talk about learning from the work at parent-teacher conferences.

2. **Expand your repertoire.**
    * Check work samples. Are multiple intelligences reflected? Adjust the curriculum. Think about if projects incorporate multiple intelligences.
    * Think about how clear learning goals and rubrics can help you and your students know and work towards expectations.
    * Encourage more student reflection. Have quick portfolio conferences. Create questions which help students reflect. Ask them to reflect on their work in writing.
    * Create a system for selecting work that might go into an end-of-year portfolio.

Figure 4–2: *First Steps in Creating a Portfolio for Every Child*

a Portfolio for Every Child

A faculty of group of teachers start...

1. **Start small, work together.**
   - Talk about portfolio purposes in grade level or faculty meetings.
   - Create a study group, read and discuss ideas.
   - Let families know that portfolios are just beginning. Enlist their help.

2. **Conduct a descriptive review of a student using observations and student work as evidence.**

3. **Find time as a faculty to discuss big ideas.**
   - Shared purposes about portfolios.
   - Multiple intelligences as a curriculum and assessment strategy that pluralizes and personalizes learning.
   - A school-wide system for creating a portfolio.
   - The uses of rubrics in standard-setting
   - How to share portfolios and projects with parents in conferences.
   - Organization of rituals for portfolio use, such as exhibitions or celebrations.

assessment, we believe that data about school and individual student performance comes from many sources. The most important data comes from teacher records and student portfolios. Standardized or state tests provide glimpses into schools and the comparison of students across a state or across the nation. These snapshots are part of the picture, but they cannot be elevated to be the most important part of the picture. The whole picture is much more like a comprehensive photo album.

The most critical data is classroom-based data that is direct, context-based, and expansive in the form of portfolios (data that records a student's learning over time). Other important information comes from data about the kind of pedagogy and curriculum offered in a school, data on the professional culture of a school, data that includes the demographics of the school, and data on communication with families. Together these different kinds of data "paint" a vivid picture of a school, its students, and its practices over time. Nothing less than this kind of closely documented and monitored system will provide the kinds of ongoing school improvement and accountability for the achievement of all our students that our schools deserve.

DATA

Primary Sources
• Student Work
• Teacher Records
Secondary Sources
• Large-Scale Tests
• Curriculum and Pedagogy
• Professional Culture
• Demographic Information
• Family Involvement

Documentation of student learning has many uses in the day-to-day life of the Cambridgeport School. Documentation alone runs the risk of being a single moment which is soon forgotten. But documentation which is used for the twin purposes of improving learning and improving teaching is rich and useful. The chart shown in Figure 4–3 describes the central focus on teacher and student while recognizing the complex factors beyond the classroom. At the same time, the chart shows the many uses of teacher records and student portfolios in serving these purposes. Although individual students and their teachers are at the heart of assessment, the development of a school-based system creates a coherent approach to assessment that provides a shared language, common organizational structures, and schoolwide rituals and procedures, which put the data to work in the service of learning.

Strategies for Assessment That Respect Multiple Ways of Documenting and Sharing Learning

Feedback

As the Cambridgeport School has grown and matured, we have continued to organize and reorganize the ways in which we systematically collect and use student work to inform learning and teaching. One of the critical elements of any system of assessment is *feedback*—the continuous loop of response to and reflection on student thinking and work in progress. Feedback that comes after completing work does little to stretch learning except for pointing out what might be tried or done differently the next time around. But continuous feedback is a powerful tool for getting smarter and smarter. It is possible to use rubrics and scoring systems with selected performances (writing, projects, etc.) or even a whole portfolio. But I believe that the greatest power in using portfolios resides in the personalization of assessment through the descriptive processes that capture thinking and performance at many

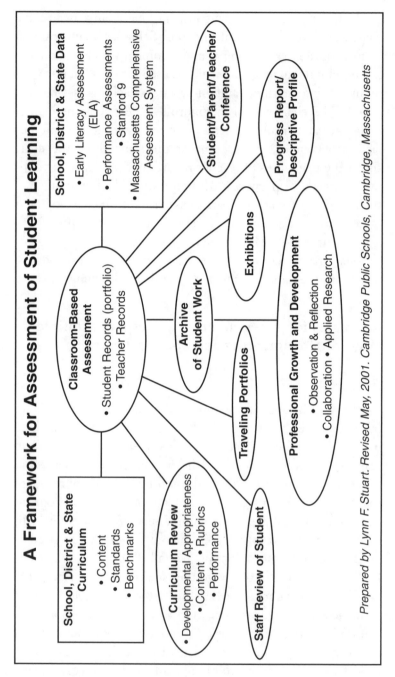

Figure 4–3: *A Framework for Assessment of Student Learning*

stages. Rubrics can create clarity about the standards set for an episode of learning or for a whole project. Rubrics can guide teacher and student to reflect on understanding and performance as they connect standards to personal goals and progress. But rubrics don't tell the whole story.

Student Reflection Guides Learning

In recent years, we have focused increasingly on the student's role in reflecting on his or her work. Teachers at every grade level have developed protocols for student self-assessment. The power to engage in meaningful work across a variety of intelligences and also to reflect on learning is as important for the child learner as it is for the adult learner. Our commitment to ongoing discussions with students about their work includes their participation in parent–teacher–student conferences. In these three-way conferences, student work is the central focus of discussion about what he or she knows and can do. In the seventh and eighth grade, Traveling Portfolios provide regular opportunities to share work with families and give parents an opportunity to respond to the portfolios.

Exhibitions and Celebrations

Curriculum exhibitions and our end-of-year Portfolio Celebration Day have become cherished rituals for sharing student achievement with families and the wider community. Exhibitions can be as simple as poetry readings or "museum" tours of the artifacts created by students in their study of a particular theme. Or they may be dazzling performances of music, dance, drama, construction, and written and visual arts projects, all blended into a magnificent evening of celebrating the rigor and joy of learning. Portfolio Celebration Day brings together the whole school in what may well be the most treasured moment of the year. It is preceded by days of reflection, conferences, and the final "editing" of what becomes the end-of-year portfolio for the school archive where it will be housed until the student graduates from eighth grade. Putting the end-of-year portfolio together is like visiting with old friends—looking at work done months ago or weeks ago, rereading, reflecting on artwork, delighting in new technologies mastered including the digital camera, and lovingly assembling the portfolio. It is a measure of learning, valued more because of the process of feedback and reflection.

Portfolio Celebration Day brings everyone to school: parents, aunts, uncles, grandparents, the central office, university friends, businesspeople, and the clergy. We invite everyone we know. No one is left out. Families read stories and are guided in questions to ask as they visit their children's classes throughout the school. It is the one time of year that kindergarten families may be reading eighth-grade autobiographies and eighth-grade families may be marveling at the wonderful fresh look at the world of a five-year-old. The day is treasured as the whole school celebrates learning together.

Graduation by Portfolio: High Stakes in a Community Setting

As our first kindergarten students approached the middle grades, we began in earnest to think about how they would demonstrate their competence by meeting an eighth-grade graduation requirement. We wanted to require eighth-grade students to engage in long-term projects in the major subject areas; to develop organizational and "executive function" skills of increasingly independent work (which also requires collaboration among peers); to produce quality demonstrations and presentations; and, last, to be able to respond to questions from a review panel of teachers, family members, and business and community guests. This graduation requirement we developed has "high stakes." Each eighth grader needs to complete the Portfolio Review in order to participate in the graduation and receive an eighth-grade certificate. The requirement is also met within a community that supports all the students and gives them time to revise, recreate, and practice their presentations before the "moment of truth" arrives. The final preparation stages also include coaching from seventh-grade assistants who help in the final presentation, providing support and gaining an awareness of the expectation that the mantle of graduation requirements will soon fall on them.

Celebrating and Protecting Student and Teacher Dignity and Learning

Curriculum exhibitions, Portfolio Celebration Day, and the Eighth-Grade Graduation Portfolio all serve an essential purpose in education. They bring acknowledgment of learning and high-quality work to a public place. Public schools need public demonstrations of what students know and can do in authentic contexts for learning—their classroom, their school, and their community. Such demonstrations value hard work, accomplishment, and sharing of skill with others. Surely, these moments instill pride in each student and family, and create more questions about what else may be learned. More importantly, these demonstrations invite public awareness of the complexity of teaching and learning that begins to reach into the communities that will "receive" these students as adult workers and community participants in the future.

Chapter 5

The Middle Elementary Years: Portfolios Become a Window into the Learner's Mind and the Teacher's Teaching
EVANGELINE HARRIS STEFANAKIS WITH
KATHLEEN GUINEE

Watching them compile their work is really a window into my teaching. I find student portfolios remind me of the work we did. As I look back at our work, I adjust what I do to meet the students' needs and the curricular guidelines.

(Sarah Fiarman)

Sarah's fifth/sixth-grade classroom at the Cambridge-port School has twenty-four students, ranging from nine- to twelve-year-olds from diverse cultural and economic family backgrounds including several who are Haitian, African American, and Puerto Rican. This group of diverse learners is with Sarah for all subject areas from 8:15 to 2:30 each day. Although a teaching assistant or student teacher may also be in the classroom for some portions of the school day, Sarah teaches all twenty-four children. Even with the large amount of time she spends with her students, Sarah admits that it is a challenge to know all individuals and to cater to each student's needs. She says, "It is definitely my responsibility to know them. It is hard to connect to each child each day." So, she works to accommodate this wide range of learners, by listening to what they say, seeing what they do, and regularly talking to them about what they are doing.

Portfolios help Sarah differentiate her teaching in response to students' differing needs because they allow her:

1. To know her students,
2. To accommodate for their individual needs, and
3. To develop more independent learners who take ownership of their learning process.

When students leave Sarah's class, she ideally wants them to be able to reflect on the process and the products of their learning. Sarah's story of her portfolio practices validates her conclusion—"Portfolios make visible my students' learning, and help me see what I am teaching!" (as shown in Figure 5–1).

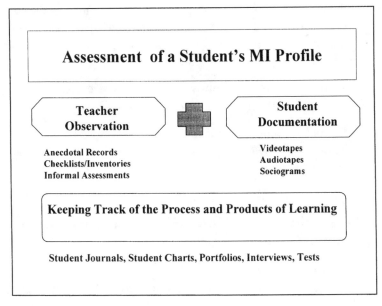

Figure 5–1: *Assessment of a Student's MI Profile*

Portfolios Represent a Way to Know Learners and to See Their Thinking

Portfolios, for Sarah and many teachers in grades 3 through 6, represent a way to know learners and to see their thinking. Sarah articulates her purposes for using portfolios as she explains how she introduces students to portfolios in the beginning of the year. As she states, portfolios are the way we constantly think about our learning. She consciously sets a context for portfolio use in her classroom.

> We talk about portfolios in the adult world during meeting time. A friend of mine is an artist and he has an artist's portfolio. Early in the year he comes to group meeting and we look at his portfolio and talk. My students see that a portfolio is a way for people to get to know who a person is through their work.

> I show students my teacher portfolio and explain how when I was applying for jobs, I needed to put together a portfolio of my own work. Then we talk as a whole class about what we could learn about someone from a portfolio. This is how we define what our portfolios are going to be about.

As Sarah suggests, portfolios are the way we (teacher and learner) constantly think about our learning:

> With older children we make our purposes for using portfolios clear. We help them see that portfolios are a vehicle for personalizing the learning process.

The Starting Point: How *Do* We Learn from a Portfolio?

Sarah introduces portfolios in the first two weeks of school and explicitly teaches her students how to collect and how to reflect on their work. Teaching students how to reflect on their work begins with modeling a reflective process for the group. For Sarah, it is a two-step process of clarifying definitions and outlining strategies for portfolio use.

We first examine adult portfolios so that the students understand their purposes and definition. We ask ourselves, how are other teachers and students going to learn from our portfolios? What can my portfolio tell others about me?

Portfolio Requirements: Collecting, Selecting, and Reflecting on Student Work

Sarah finds that she needs to teach a series of minilessons about how to make a portfolio system work. This explicit initial teaching allows students to take ownership of the process and work more independently. Skillfully, she uses work samples to teach students about collecting, selecting, and reflecting on their work. Sarah teaches about the reflective process by creating a piece of reflective writing, which she purposely has written ambiguously. She explains that the class examines the artwork and reflects on it:

> We look at work and we think aloud about what we see.
>
> I ask them which piece of artwork, from the two I show, goes with my reflection. My students can't tell because the reflection says, "I worked hard on this." It sounds like what my students write on their reflection sheets—"I worked hard on it, I put a lot of effort into it, I think I did a really good job on it."
>
> They quickly see that what I wrote could be talking about any piece of artwork. Then, I ask them to figure out what else I could have said to be more specific about just this piece of work. Together we write about a piece of artwork and describe what we see.
>
> My students come up with wonderful ideas. They ask me questions like why did the artist decide to paint something green in this place? Why did they decide to put this color in the center? I think this gets them in the mood of thinking about their work, examining the thought process behind the creation process.

Explore how Emma and others work on reflection on the CD-ROM.

Portfolio Selections Are Clues About Students and Their Personal Issues

According to Sarah, each piece of work a student wants to save is a clue about where powerful learning experiences have occurred for them. Portfolios help her students see that they are selecting certain types of work, and omitting other types. Over time Sarah has noticed these omissions are a clue to areas of challenge for that child.

> Another way for me to know my students emerges when they are choosing work. Often, I notice that they haven't chosen anything from a particular curricular area. That helps me to see that this is an area that either they didn't produce in or they don't feel as confident in. They say, "I don't like any of my science pieces," so for me as a teacher that's sort of a red flag.

Sarah and her teaching team find that portfolios for students in grades 3, 4, and 5, especially for students who have learning challenges, chronicle what is meaningful and important to them in their learning process. Students who struggle the whole year still find something in their portfolios that they feel proud of. Sarah recalls a story about Teddy, a student who came into the class reading poorly and not writing at all:

> At the beginning of his second year, we started studying poetry in my class. Teddy said, "Can I show them my portfolio that has all my poetry in it from last year?" So he pulled his portfolio and showed it to the whole class before we started working on poems. It was really moving to me that he remembered that the poetry was in his portfolio and that it had samples of what was important to him.

Portfolios are a vehicle for students who struggle to find evidence of their abilities, as with Teddy. Everyone, as Sarah recounts, has a challenge area, and for students with learning disabilities there are many. Yet a portfolio shows students' unique multiple intelligences in different work samples. Seeing what Jonathan, a child with learning disabilities, does on projects helped him take ownership of his challenges and work to improve them.

See samples from Jonathan's portfolio on the CD–ROM.

84

Portfolios Are a Window into the Learner's Mind and the Teacher's Teaching

Sarah thinks portfolios are an enormously beneficial tool for teachers to reflect on their practices by looking at students' work.

> When we're assembling the portfolio, I start to reflect on my own practice. I notice that we don't have many art pieces to choose from. What does that say about my teaching? It's very focused on writing and math.

> Next, the student work showed me the math samples and I saw that the work was too full of computation. As a teacher, I need to be doing more open-ended tasks, asking problem-solving questions and doing inquiry-based work.

Sarah had an epiphany about her mathematics teaching in one of our conversations about portfolios. As she realized, portfolios help teachers examine what they teach and how they teach.

> Portfolios offer a way for teachers not to go the whole year to see what else they could be doing. Portfolios are an ongoing teacher assessment, a way to think about our self-correction. Portfolios allow me to be more inclusive and accountable in what I teach and how I teach.

> It's enormously powerful when my students are putting together their portfolio books mid-year and at the end of the year. They're so proud of them. That's a good time for me to reflect on my year's teaching and what I need to do differently next year. Through portfolios I process our work together over the whole year. I'm not quite sure how else I might do that, if not with a portfolio.

Portfolios Show Growth for Both Students and Teachers

Sarah believes that to make portfolios meaningful, showcasing work that demonstrates student growth is essential to document progress.

Can you take September and November work samples and see the differences in spelling, in punctuation, in content, and in organization? Absolutely!

She asks students to select work that demonstrates how they learned a skill or how they improved in a particular area. Sarah, looking at Laura's portfolio, sees that students in grade 5 are old enough to identify which work samples demonstrate personal growth.

> We select portfolio pieces by looking at the dates of work and comparing what happens over time. We are noting where our work shows a difference—where there's been growth. Students select pieces from September, when they were putting two-thirds of an idea down on paper, to work in November in which they are able to walk us through a very complete idea.

Portfolios, for Sarah and for her students, are clear evidence of growth and learning. *Compare Dany and Emma's portfolios from September to May on the CD-ROM.*

Portfolios Are for Students, Teachers, Parents, and Community Members

Clarifying the purposes and the audiences for portfolios is vital for all members of a school community. Is the portfolio for the teacher as a record of work completion, for the school as evidence of material taught, or for the student as evidence of learning and growth? Depending on the audience, the portfolios may look different because they are addressing different learning goals. At the Cambridgeport School, the audience for portfolios may be multifaceted, but ultimately the portfolio belongs to the child. Sarah clarifies for students that the portfolio procedure is designed to demonstrate *their* personal growth in many domains:

> I start by telling the students that this is going to be part of a beautiful book that we're going to put together about *you*. Then, I show portfolios from the previous years' students to demonstrate how growth in skills and abilities is demonstrated over each month.

The audiences for portfolios can be seen as a series of concentric circles, which represent the stakeholders who care about student learning, starting with the student, then the teacher, the parent, other teachers, the school community, and the district (see Figure 5–2). The portfolio makes student work visible to the community as evidence of teaching and learning in a school and in each classroom.

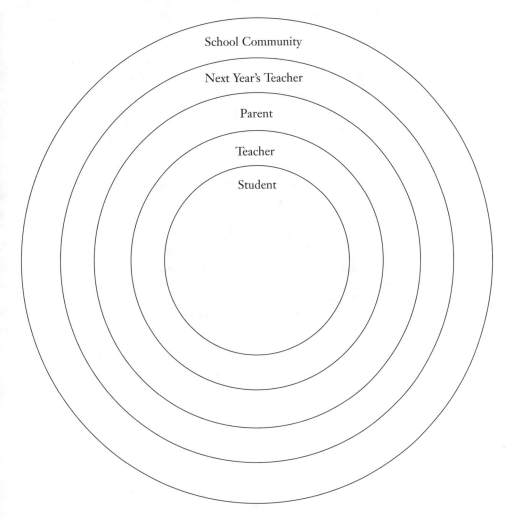

Figure 5–2: *Audiences/Purposes for Portfolio (created in collaboration with Steve Seidel 1995)*

Portfolios and Student Work Make Teachers Accountable for Teaching All Students

Sarah believes in telling students that portfolios are evidence of their learning and a place they can preserve samples of their work for future readers. The portfolio is a book that compiles their work and chronicles it over a year. As we can see in Emma's portfolio on the CD-ROM, each entry shows that her writing, drawing, and mathematics skills are improving:

> Even the idea that they're working toward building a book helps students understand the portfolio's meaning. Then it doesn't feel like some silly hoop that the teacher is making students jump through. Have them see the end product, a sample of a portfolio that shows students new learning and evidence of growth. Let them know where they're headed.

How to Organize and Manage Portfolios in the Middle Elementary Years

Sarah and her teaching team have worked diligently to address the nitty-gritty logistics of managing portfolios in large classes. Sarah outlines her five-step process for a portfolio system that allows her to keep the process manageable:

1. **Collection**: We start with hanging files and a checklist to guide our collection.

   > Initially, I didn't have a selection checklist and my students started making it on their own, keeping track themselves. It was a great idea for tracking samples that came from them, a way to systematically see that all subjects were there.

   > We have hanging files where they put their work that's considered portfolio possibilities. We have a colored file folder in their hanging file where they put their reflections. They can keep track of the work sample and what they've reflected on using key tools—a selection checklist, a reflection sheet with guiding questions, and plastic sleeves to display final work samples.

The checklist, which evolved from the student suggestions, has a notation for including their rough draft of the piece. They are expected to include both the rough and final drafts. I find that rough drafts are important so we can see a child's writing and editing process.

2. **Selection**: We examine the quality of our work and decide what to display.

> I help my students get clear that their selections are a compilation of their work. The process of putting together a portfolio is a big one so I break it up into smaller pieces. Each time they finish selecting work and doing a reflection, they get a plastic sleeve. They put the work in the sleeve and it's ready.

3. **A Selection Rubric**: We cull quality work into portfolio folders and create a filing system.

> How could I involve the students in looking for quality work samples to put in the portfolio? A rubric suggests, I'm going to view these pieces of work according to criteria. We are looking for work that shows evidence of clear ideas, personal opinions, and scientific thinking. How would they assess their own work themselves?

The Project Rubric is available on the CD-ROM.

In Sarah's classroom, student work in the pass-along portfolio is selected in a three-stage process.

1. All student work is collected in folders by subject.
2. Students periodically identify some pieces from their folders as portfolio possibilities and place them in hanging files in a separate file cabinet.
3. Finally, students select the items for their final portfolios from their "portfolio possibilities" files.

4. **Selecting** portfolio possibilities and then portfolio finalists.

> I'm thinking of having two hanging file spaces—having the filing cabinet just be a general place for work and then using the bottom drawers for the portfolio finalists. At the end of the year they're just pulling out of the finalist drawers, always narrowing down.

5. **Compiling the Portfolio Book:** Creating a cover that is a finished self-portrait.

The beautiful self-portraits are key to personalizing the work! We put about a month's work into making the self-portrait. It's something that the children have invested enormous energy in and they're gorgeous. That's an enormous incentive.

As Sarah and her students know, portfolios are meaningful ways to showcase student learning and reflection for individuals and groups in a classroom environment.

Sarah's Class: A Portfolio Environment for Individual and Group Learning (with Kathleen Guinee)*

Sarah's classroom has a clutter-free, organized feeling. Student artwork about collaboration lines the walls above the bulletin boards. One piece has a picture of a plant with three branching flowers and reads, "My class grows like a flower because we learn a lot and our brains grow." *Look on the CD-ROM for classroom photos.*

A bulletin board in the back of the room contains photographs and essays about a class trip students took to climb Mt. Monadnock in New Hampshire. A Revolutionary War time line runs along the side wall, above the cubbies. Like Bela's room, Sarah's room has a rug, although it covers a smaller area. The rug is located at the back of the room, in front of the field-trip bulletin board. For meeting and class discussions, some of the students sit directly on the rug with their backs against the wall. The front of the room features a blackboard on the wall, six rectangular tables—half positioned lengthwise and half positioned widthwise—and a teacher's desk. Sarah's classroom provides an environment for students to share as a group, and to display independent and collaborative work (see Figure 5–3).

---

*This excerpt is adapted from a paper written by Kathleen Guinee, research assistant and doctoral candidate at Harvard Graduate School of Education, in conjunction with the course work of T-160 Understanding Learning Challenges taught by Dr. Evangeline Harris Stefanakis (December 2000).

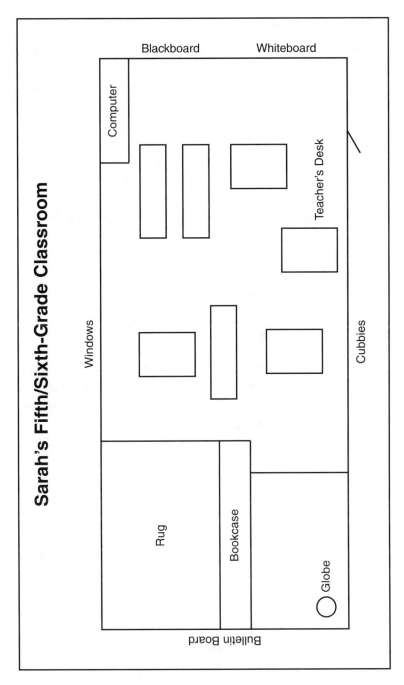

Figure 5–3: *Sarah's Fifth/Sixth-Grade Classroom*

Reflection in Everyday Classroom Practice—Math

The following story shows not only how Sarah incorporates multiple intelligences instruction into her math class, but also how one student is conscious of and openly verbal about reflection. Sarah and Donald, the assistant teacher, take the fifth graders to the computer room down the hall to learn about geometry using GeoLogo. One student carries a crate of orange math folders from Sarah's classroom. These folders contain the fifth graders' math sheets and their math journals, bound notebooks with blue covers.

Sarah incorporates the use of multiple intelligences into the math lessons, namely logical-mathematical, bodily-kinesthetic, visual-spatial, and interpersonal. One morning, to introduce the students to a new set of GeoLogo commands, Sarah impersonated the Logo turtle. Through a collaborative effort, the students gave commands, specifying a combination of turns and steps to get Sarah from her position in the front of the room to out the door at the side of the room. The students took turns "moving" Sarah, each giving one command. Moesha volunteered to record the instructions class members gave on the whiteboard as the students directed Sarah around the furniture and out of the room.

Another way that Sarah incorporates the bodily-kinesthetic intelligence into math class is by using her body to show angles to the students. She shows students how to use their arms to make angles: one arm out to the side and one straight ahead for 90 degrees, one arm out to each side for 180 degrees, and so on. When the students have questions about how large or small to make an angle or when they struggle with calculating the difference in size between angles, Sarah has them use their arms to help answer the questions.

During math class, the students work in pairs at the computers lining the four walls of the computer classroom. Sarah challenges them to use GeoLogo to draw geometric shapes. One day, their specific task was to write a computer program that would draw three different types of triangles, and then print them with the angles labeled. After the students completed this task, Sarah gathered them for a discussion about triangles. As Sarah and the class were discussing equilateral triangles, Moesha raised her hand and asked, "Shouldn't the turns be equal if the sides are equal?" Sarah asked the class what they thought was the answer to Moesha's question. Sarah suggested that each of the three tables of students should look at the triangles they had printed to see whether both the angles and the sides were equal. Some of the students discovered that the angles on their equilateral triangles were all equal, but the numbers on their printouts were not because they had not returned the turtle to its starting direction.

After the students presented their findings, Emma raised her hand and said, "If you want to put that in your portfolio, you could include a note explaining why two numbers are the same and one is different." After further discussion around this topic, she added, "You could put it in your reflection."

Portfolios Help Teachers See Multiple Intelligences and Learning Challenges

Sarah, through portfolio work, consciously introduces MI theory to her students. She does this by examining a piece of student work in art or social studies deliberately selected to focus on an area often not acknowledged as intelligence. She explains that reading and math are not the only evidence of how people are unique or smart:

> As we look at work, they realize that we're interested in their thinking, not just about their right or wrong answers. Often in writing and math, my students assume there's a right and wrong answer. With art, they're open to the idea that there are multiple ways for products to turn out. It's a way of beginning to understand multiple intelligences for all of us.

As she reads students' reflections, Sarah learns more about what is meaningful to each individual; the reflections help her learn more about their interests and preferences. Sarah is beginning to construct MI profiles of her students.

> In a reflection on her artwork, a child said, "I really loved this, it was the first piece where I felt like I drew a tree the way it really looks." Then there is a child excited about being able to draw branches, who always wanted to draw a tree branch. That visual sense is vital to him.

Looking at student work and listening to what students say about their work helps Sarah identify strengths and specific areas of challenge. Early in the year, Sarah starts with learning that is very personal. Later, she helps students see that they are achieving standards, again by looking at samples of students' required work products.

In response to state curricular frameworks, Sarah designs her lessons around a planning question. The essential questions help her frame a way of thinking for her students (see Figure 5–4).

Incorporating the State Curriculum—Revolutionary Projects

Sarah uses multiple intelligences and interdisciplinary projects to address material from the state curriculum frameworks. For example, her fifth/sixth-grade students studied the U.S. Revolutionary era as outlined in their assignment sheets *(shown on the CD-ROM)*. Eventually, these projects were presented to parents. For the first half of the presentation, the students, dressed as Revolutionary heroes with personal biographies and diaries, sat behind the tables facing the center of the classroom. The parents milled around in the center of the **U**, reading the diary entries and examining artifacts made.

Assignment Sheets and photos of Revolutionary projects are on the CD-ROM.

Producing the Revolutionary displays involved several intelligences. For example, a student-drawn portrait of a "character" on the cover of each laminated construction paper folder represents the visual-spatial and bodily-kinesthetic intelligence.

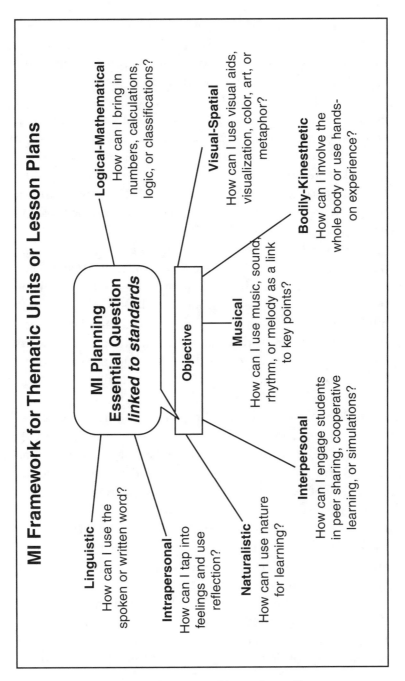

Figure 5–4: *MI Framework for Thematic Units or Lesson Plans*

Some of these drawings displayed not only the character portrayed in the project, but also the character's context, such as the tavern owned by the character's father. The contents of the folders, diary entries from the characters, involved both the linguistic and intrapersonal intelligences. The first few diary entries were from the Revolutionary time frame including at least one historically-significant event. The final entry was from the character after time-traveling to the present. In addition to the folder, each project contained two artifacts, one from Revolutionary times and one from the present. Each artifact was labeled with its name, year, the materials it was made of, and its purpose.

The collection of artifacts demonstrated creativity on the part of the students. Some students constructed their own eighteenth-century artifacts. One student made a medicine bottle out of clay. A second student made a fireplace by placing fake wood and flames in a shoebox, while another baked a sponge-cake dessert with his mother. The present-day artifacts students brought were equally diverse, including a skateboard, bicycle, toy cars, a green plastic cup for drinking milk (to go with the sponge cake), a baseball bat, and a baseball glove.

During the first half of the presentation, the students displayed their diaries and artifacts for their parents. The parents tapped into their own multiple intelligences as they viewed the artwork, read the diary entries, and looked at and touched the artifacts. The parents asked the students questions about their characters' "experiences" and about how they selected the artifacts. The students seemed very confident about sharing their work. The few concerns the students had seemed to revolve around seating order and how they should staple their diary entries into their folders.

To conclude, the students read excerpts from their diaries so that the parents could hear "words from the kids' writing in their voices," as Sarah described it. The presentation finished with a song entitled "The War of Independence" that five students wrote. As Sarah states, she can see in the collection of student work and in the curriculum projects evidence of the multiple intelligences in each individual.

Portfolios are both a window into each student's emerging capabilities, and an analytic tool for me to use so I can reach every child by reflecting on my own teaching!

Activities in Revolutionary Presentations Use the Different Intelligences	
Intelligence Areas Combined	**Activity**
Linguistic/Kinesthetic/ Interpersonal	Written diary entries Verbal presentation of excerpts
Logical-Mathematical/ Visual-Spatial	Timelines and maps
Naturalistic/Logical-Mathematical	Identified materials of artifacts
Visual-Spatial/Bodily-Kinesthetic	Drawing of character on project cover
Musical/Linguistic	Song
Bodily-Kinesthetic/Interpersonal/ Intrapersonal	Artifacts from Revolutionary times and present
Interpersonal/Linguistic/ Visual-Spatial	Presentation of projects to parents Diary entries in which other characters interacted with other characters from class
Intrapersonal/Interpersonal/ Linguistic	Diary entries for a character during both Revolutionary times and present Selection of past and present artifacts

Chapter 6

Traveling Portfolios for Adolescents: A Window for All in the Middle School Years

EVANGELINE HARRIS STEFANAKIS WITH
JILL HARRISON BERG

*As children enter adolescence, they no longer come skipping
home from school with stories about their day or with work to
hang on the fridge. This does not mean that they do not want,
or even need, to talk about their schoolwork. Adolescents thrive
when their hard work is noticed and appreciated in a portfolio.*

(Jill Harrison Berg)

In this chapter, I tell the story of Jill Harrison Berg,
a seventh- and eighth-grade teacher of humanities at the Cambridgeport School, to illustrate how multiple intelligences
theory and portfolios are particularly effective in working with
adolescents. For the past seven years, Jill has been experiment-
ing with classroom assessment based on the theory of multiple
intelligences. She is a member of a team of five middle-school
teachers of different subjects, who all see portfolios as essential
tools for documenting students' work and teachers' work.

Jill's class, like the school, represents a myriad of backgrounds:
a multicultural population, 51 percent majority and 49 percent
minority, based on the Cambridge urban school desegregation
formula. Her students represent a wide range of class, race, and
ethnic backgrounds. A high proportion of students in her school
are English language learners or have special educational needs,
so their reading skills range from third to tenth grade.

Jill, as a humanities teacher, is more than a teacher of her subject. She thinks deeply about who her students are and what they bring to the learning environment every day. Two key goals emerge as Jill describes what she sees as the unique challenge of being a middle-school educator. Her first goal is to know the whole child through his or her work, applying MI theory to help students know themselves as learners.

> I believe that during this critical period of identity development and preparation for more demanding academic studies, I must guide students to become aware of their own learning styles and habits. They must become aware of all of the ways they are smart. This knowledge can provide a solid foundation for them as they begin the adolescent process of deciding *who they are* and *who they want to be.*

Her second goal is to find ways to exhibit the variety of learning experiences that her students have, to counteract the fact that they are not bringing work home and don't allow their parents to come to school. For Jill, reaching her students as individuals means enriching the interactions between students, teachers, and parents.

> I feel I must ensure that students' conversations with their families about school remain ongoing and interactive despite the adolescent tendency to avoid dialogue with parents.

Portfolios Help Teachers See the Whole Student and His or Her Multiple Intelligences

As Jill suggests, portfolios help middle-school teachers to collaboratively assess and teach their students by examining a collection of work from different subjects:

> Portfolios help us as teachers share what happens in our class-rooms. Portfolios make us look at what we were trying to do, and what the student in question produced. So the portfolio provides the starting point for talking about students and thinking about different multiple intelligences in each individual, especially those who are a puzzle to many of us.

In middle school it is not always easy for teachers to know their students. Typically, departmentalized teachers see their students for one subject and know them only in terms of their interest and performance in that subject. As Jill reminds us:

> Many middle-school teachers in a departmentalized program do not have the opportunity to see their students in a variety of academic and nonacademic roles. Instead of having one classroom of learners to keep track of, departmentalized teachers typically have more than one hundred students. The important work of developing an MI profile on middle-school students—knowing their strengths and how to build on them—is slightly impeded.
>
> When we use portfolios, all of a child's teachers can view his or her accomplishments throughout the school on a regular basis and learn about each student's individual strengths. For the teaching team, the portfolio is an invaluable tool for working together to develop an MI profile—identifying strengths and how to teach to them.

As Jill suggests, at the middle-school level, teachers need to know more about the array of their students' abilities. Jill explains how portfolios and MI theory help her to understand her students better and to see multiple ways to engage them in learning.

> Portfolios allow me to learn about the work that my students produce for their other subjects/teachers. If students are given the latitude and materials to develop projects that demonstrate skills in a variety of modes, then multiple intelligences are demonstrated in the work of portfolios.
>
> For me, portfolios provide a vehicle for reflection and exhibition of MI-based projects. It is up to the teacher to allow kids to explore and demonstrate their multiple intelligences.
>
> The portfolios are also an important awareness tool for the teacher's own professional development, as they help the teacher notice what kinds of opportunities for products and performances she is giving students and how to best adapt the curriculum to serve her students' needs.

For middle-school students, according to Jill, portfolios offer a means for demonstrating a student's multiple intelligences:

If you had looked only at MCAS (Massachusetts Comprehensive Assessment System) test scores of last year's eighth-grade class, you would have thought these students were in trouble. Many of them were working on adaptive programs in special education and their results on this "comprehensive assessment test" might suggest that they lack any skills that society values.

Throughout the year, these same students were able to use portfolios to demonstrate to themselves and others what they knew in four subject areas: math, English/language arts, science, and history/social studies.

The written text of some of their math projects might have seemed confusing, but when they stood up and answered questions about the velocity of racing cars, for example, they were able to explain velocity as clearly as day. They knew what velocity meant and they were able to take two cars and demonstrate the concept.

Students could use knowledge. Does this always show on a written test? Using portfolios makes it so clear—kids are smart in so many different ways. During their portfolio presentations, I was impressed by how articulate these kids were about what they knew.

I could see them in the future working in businesses, being managers or corporate trainers making presentations. They are so personable; they're such people-people. When you look only at their test scores, you do not see what else they can be. Portfolios provide a reminder of what is really important in life—being able to demonstrate what you know in real situations as we see in Riana's, Susan's and Louis' portfolio.

Look on the CD-ROM for the portfolio presentations by Riana, Susan, and Louis.

Are middle-school students typically aware of their multiple intelligences or even focused on understanding their capabilities? Are most students taking ownership of their learning process during the middle-school years—with parents and teachers working together on their behalf? Or, to achieve high standards, are schools increasingly taking control of what students learn at exactly the time when students want to take control of who they are and what they do? I would agree with Jill—it is unfortunate that in middle school the demands to meet standards and to cover the curriculum mean that learning often becomes more teacher-driven and textbook-driven and focused on mastering subject-area content. As Jill reminds us:

> Traditionally in the middle school, the teacher is the real coordinator of a student's learning process, while other educational stakeholders such as guardians, family members, and counselors may contribute to the conversation.

What tools can help students take a more active role in their own learning? How can students and parents work together with teachers toward high standards to assess academic achievement?

Traveling Portfolios Help Students Take Ownership of Their Learning

Jill suggests that the main purpose for using portfolios is to encourage students to work toward high standards and also to take ownership of their learning. The control over the learning process, and the power to provide evidence of achieving high standards, moves from the teachers to the learners. As she explains:

> Adolescents do not like to be told what to do. They must be involved in the decision-making if they are to take ownership of their learning. If we include adolescents in the parent-teacher communication loop around portfolios, the student begins to regard the teacher and the parent as allies who can assist them in achieving their goals and meeting the standards.

> Portfolio activities (such as conferences and report cards) which are intended to report on and improve student progress, must include the student so they feel that they have control over that progress.

Every student in Jill's class has his or her own academic challenges, and careful monitoring of progress is crucial so that the student owns this hard work along with the teacher.

> When classroom successes occur, adolescents need to be empowered to share and celebrate them with those adults who are supporting them. When classroom challenges are identified, students need to feel open to working with this support team to be a part of developing a solution.

To foster student ownership, Jill presents her model of "Traveling Portfolios"—a documentation and assessment process designed around four important goals:

1. To collect evidence of students achieving standards and curriculum benchmarks.
2. To show the diversity of what students know and can do.
3. To foster regular communication about progress between students, teachers, and parents.
4. To help students see how they are smart, and how they learn.

Traveling Portfolios provide a variety of evidence about what the student knows and can do. This evidence serves as a focal point for conferences, as support for comments on a progress report, and/or as an entry point for ongoing interactive communication with parents about students' work. When students learn that the work in their Traveling Portfolios can play an important role in their learning, they begin to take greater ownership of their learning and are motivated to do their best.

Traveling Portfolios: A Description of the Process

Jill outlines the Traveling Portfolio process in a series of five steps.

Steps to Implementing Traveling Portfolios

1. Students keep work that has been passed back throughout the year. Every six to eight weeks, they choose exemplary work from various subject areas.
2. Students reflect on selected pieces of work using a Portfolio Work Tag (See Figure 6–1).
3. Students write a cover letter to family members. Student work and the cover letter are sent home in specially created portfolio folders to signal their work is special.
4. Family member(s) have about one week to examine the work, talk about it with their child, and write a note in response to the cover letter.
5. The teacher files the returned work (and letters) in an archive for the end-of-the-year portfolio.

In the following list, Jill more completely describes, in her words, her strategies for managing Traveling Portfolios in her classroom:

1. Every six to eight weeks, students browse through recently completed and returned work to select products or performances that will be sent home.

   In my class students are guided in choosing one or two pieces from each academic area, as well as one or two nonacademic artifacts, such as a tape of a trombone recital, minutes from a student council meeting, or even photos of a playground feat. This collection of work, taken together, provides a vivid picture of each child's many intelligences, skills, and interests.

2. Students reflect on the individual pieces of work using a Work Tag.

   Most middle-school students have strong enough writing skills that they do not need someone literally "sitting beside" them to guide them through the reflection process. A template such as the Portfolio Work Tag can guide students through this reflective process on their own.

   This worksheet poses questions designed to help students recognize when they have created quality work, what kinds of habits help them feel proud of their work, and how they can produce work they will be proud of in the future. This can be challenging for students who have not yet developed a habit of self-reflection; students' self-reflections do become more genuine and meaningful with practice. Once mastered, thoughtful student responses, prompted by this reflection sheet, will give parents, teachers, and the students themselves important insight into the child as a learner.

3. Each student writes a cover letter to his or her parents or family members that explains their role. Parents look over the contents of the portfolio, discuss the work with their children, and then write a letter back to the child. X

Portfolio Work Tag

Name _____

_____   _____

    Date of assignment or project   Today's date

Reflecting Back

* What was the assignment? Describe what you were supposed to do or make. Were there other parts to the assignment?

_____

_____

_____

_____

_____

_____

* How did you do or make it? How did you get the idea or answer? Did you have a strategy? What did you do first? Second? What materials did you use?

_____

_____

_____

_____

_____

_____

_____

Figure 6–1: *Portfolio Work Tag (developed by Jill Harrison Berg)*

Self-reflecting
* Did the assignment turn out the way you wanted? Did you have a goal? What did you judge it by?

_____

_____

_____

_____

_____

* What do you think this work says or shows about you?

_____

_____

_____

_____

* Did you choose to include this piece of work in your portfolio? _____ yes _____ no

Looking Ahead
* What would you change if you did or made this again? How would you have approached this project differently? What would you like to improve on or add?

_____

_____

_____

_____

_____

Figure 6–1: *Continued*

As families become familiar with Traveling Portfolios throughout the school year, the cover letter does not need to describe the portfolio routine; it becomes more personalized and includes student observations and reflections on the collection of work. (When literacy is an issue, parents are asked to simply sign the bottom of the letter.)

4. Students gather their work, reflection sheets, and cover letters in special Traveling Portfolio folders they have made, and take the portfolios home for one week.

Students may keep their portfolios at home for about one week, allowing parents, regardless of their work schedules or routines, to spend quality time with the portfolio. Portfolio folders should be designed with some thickness, to accommodate evidence in a variety of formats: computer disk, video, journals, etc.

5. When students return the portfolios, I, as the teacher, pore over their contents.

I take note of which parents require an immediate response and others with whom I may wish to touch base during regular conferences.

After reviewing each returned portfolio folder, I file the work in a hanging file folder box.

This collection of culled work is a useful resource at the end of the year for student self-evaluation and for compiling student portfolios for our school's permanent archive.

Traveling Portfolios: A Window for All Teachers, Parents, and Students

While Traveling Portfolios provide a window for teachers and parents into the middle-school learners and their learning, they also provide a window for the teacher into her own teaching and into the families of the students she works with. Looking at student work collections, teachers can assess:

- the effectiveness of their written feedback on the work
- the kinds of assignments that make the student proud
- the variety of assignments that they are giving.

At the same time, parents who view the student's work in the portfolio can learn about the types of assignments and feedback that the student has been receiving in school. As Jill notes, one parent responded to his daughter's Traveling Portfolio with a letter to the student that was interlaced with comments for Jill:

Dear Riana,

1. Constellation essay: well written! Let's learn what the zodiac constellations are—why are they special to all the others?

2. MFA book: *Nice job, Jill!*

    a. Fun to read and look at! It makes me want to learn more about the Bronze and Iron Ages—I didn't know they overlapped with Classical Greece.

    b. Correct spelling on: perfume, widely

    Q: Do they ever write in cursive? (Or is it required?)

3. Sunapee mountain page: It brings me there! This is enjoyable to read because you have gone over it and improved it before calling it finished.

    Q: Can you stress in the writing: less use of slang and less use of sentences which sound like a child talking (as would be written in, for example, a script for a play)?

This response vividly reveals that, as students, they take ownership of learning, and so do parents.

Reflection Is a Key to Portfolios: Using the Work Tag

The Portfolio Work Tag is another resource for keeping track of learning, and for noting improvement. As Jill describes:

> After selecting portfolio pieces to save, the student completes a written reflection exercise for the assignments he or she has chosen. This Portfolio Work Tag guides the student in reflecting on what makes good work, what makes him or her proud, and how to improve his or her work.
>
> This reflection sheet also communicates to parents and teachers what the student feels they have learned from an assignment and how the student feels about the quality of his or her own work. The Portfolio Work Tags turn the Traveling Portfolios into an effective, qualitative assessment system that naturally takes students through the process of self-assessment and setting learning goals.

The design of the Portfolio Work Tag is based on four stages of reflection (Seidel 1997) which include reflecting back, reflecting inward, reflecting outward, and reflecting forward. These stages help the student to recall the purposes and goals of the assignment, to assess their own work based on those goals, and to set specific new learning goals for themselves. The Portfolio Work Tag was designed by Jill and her team for grade 7/8.

Reflection

The key to authentic self-assessment and developing student ownership is guiding students to reflect on their work. The essential components of reflection are:

- Looking back
- Looking inward
- Looking outward
- Looking forward

(From *Portfolio Practices*. Steve Seidel, 1997, Harvard Project Zero.)

Portfolio Cover Letters: Parents and Students (and Teachers) Talk on Paper

Over three years, Jill has found that the cover letters and the parents' responses play an important role in opening the dialogue about student work among the students, parents, and teachers. As she so aptly suggests:

> This letter, which students write to their family members to introduce the Traveling Portfolio, reminds parents that although children don't always act like it and will rarely say it, they do care what parents think about their work. It provides students with a much-needed and desired excuse to show their parents their work.

Jill shares a few hints on how to create parent cover letters:

Cover Letter

The cover letter is the key to drawing family members in. Be sure students' letters follow these guidelines:

1. Contain an address to specific person/people.
2. Explain what Traveling Portfolios are and how they work.
3. Explain what is in the portfolio and why.
4. Explain what the family member is expected to do.
5. Note the due date, underlined or circled.
6. Use proper letter format (why not provide this regular practice?).
7. Check that the letter is neat, clean, and carefully proofread.

When parents write letters in response to these cover letters, according to Jill, they have the opportunity to respond to their children with support or praise of their work. Sometimes parents ask questions about the assignments, and sometimes they make notes about areas in which they hope the student will continue to improve. Parents, Jill has observed, frequently

111

respond to her as well. They write notes about how much they enjoy seeing the student's work, sometimes adding questions or concerns about student progress, along with questions about the curriculum activity, often suggesting ideas or resources. The following sample parent responses to the cover letter show the diversity of relationships.

From one parent . . .

Dear L.,

I want to tell you again, like I did at the dinner table, that I am proud of you, and have lots of great respect for your positive attitude towards all of your classes and for your understanding that it is through hard work that we get places and move forward in life. You are strong, your energy is bright like the sun, and you bring happiness to our lives. Thank you my love—

Love you, Mama

P.S. I am so amazed at your artwork, like always!!!

From another parent . . . focused on academics

Dear D.,

I can see you'll be doing higher-level stuff in seventh grade. I'm impressed with the math and science assignments because they are showing you the importance of patience and attention to the details.

The reading assignments are great, too, because they are giving you the opportunity to express yourself a little more. You should keep up this work. Write what you really think. You can't learn to write and speak well without plenty of practice. Write with confidence and don't worry about how it looks. That will get better with practice.

Love, Dad

When portfolios are returned, as noted earlier, Jill always pores over the contents. The parent responses, whether directed to the student or to Jill as the teacher, can tell her a lot. They directly and indirectly communicate information about a family's priorities, concerns, educational background, and relationships. As Jill contends:

> Cover letters often help me understand the relationship between parent and child. They may indicate something about the background or the native language of the family.

> Parents typically respond to students with praise of the work, questions about assignments, or notes about areas to which they hope the child will give more attention.

Along with a letter to the student, parents often write unsolicited letters to Jill, sharing what they observe at home.

From a parent whose schedule makes it impossible for her to come in:

Dear Jill,

As a parent and a lifelong learner, I must tell you that I am thrilled with A.'s latest portfolio. The progress she has made in between portfolios is excellent. Clearly the subject matter you teach has inspired and motivated A. to start really pushing in her quest for more knowledge.

This portfolio demonstrates that she is now ready to bring and nurture her zest for knowledge far into her future and hopefully for a lifetime.

(Signed by the parent)

From a parent whose home language is not English:

From who it concerns.

Dear teacher, when I review B.'s works, I think you doing a very good job. B's doing fine, but I hope he's doing better. Keep focus doing he's homework.

(signed by the parent)

To get a sense of the individual stories in Traveling Portfolios, please see the CD and look at the student work of Riana, Sarah, and Louis comparing and contrasting their work.

Family Conferencing and Grading with Portfolios

Jill also describes how portfolios support grading and graduation according to standards. Jill is very clear about her rationale for grading, which includes a report card and the Traveling Portfolio as part of a comprehensive assessment system.

> If we are operating from the premise that all students are smart in different ways, then we must accept that traditional report cards and standardized testing alone will not do. These practices communicate to parents and students an unfair judgment about whether the student is or is not smart. While we know that recognizing all intelligences is important, accountability is important as well. Parents, students, teachers, and even local real estate agents need proof that learning is occurring in our schools.

> Report cards are based on a narrow set of intelligences. They traditionally have space for letter grades in five or six academic areas, and possibly a few lines for teacher comments. A thoughtful teacher can work to provide a true assessment of a student's progress in these five or six narrowly defined areas, but this is only a small part of the true story. How can a student's musical, interpersonal, or kinesthetic strengths be included? The report card is truly incomplete until it is accompanied by a Traveling Portfolio, a collection of work that contains evidence of achievement in a variety of intelligences.

When Traveling Portfolios are a part of conference and reporting procedures, a variety of evidence is available to support the narrow, but required, reports about what students know and are able to do.

Family portfolio conferences, according to Jill, are an opportunity for all educational stakeholders to *sit beside* one another and discuss student work.

> These thirty-minute portfolio conferences are scheduled to take place twice a year and always include the student, parent, and

teacher, as well as others such as unified arts teachers, counselors, tutors, grandparents, etc. Ideally, parents have already spent a week examining the portfolio work, and teachers have had a hand in compiling it, so they are all familiar with it. The conference is an opportunity to voice observations and have a conversation about the work.

To help focus the conference on specific questions, a protocol is used (see Figure 6–2). Jill goes on to describe:

> We use the "Conference Goals" sheet to clearly note our observations and new goals. It helps us to determine what each of us can do—the student, the parents, and the teacher—to support the student in setting and achieving new learning goals and what each party will do toward achieving these goals. We look at specific assignments the student has identified as work he or she is proud of. We ask, what is it? How was it produced? What does it show about the student as an individual and as a learner? And what can we do to help the student to be this proud of all of his or her work? As we work together to discover what makes this individual student proud, we are all learning what we can do to help the child to be a motivated learner.

With this technique, grading and assessment can be a learning experience as it is in Jill's class and all classes at the Cambridgeport School.

> Assessment is most valuable when it provides real evidence of what the student knows and is able to do. When we have a clear idea of what students' strengths are, we can help students develop strategies to use their strengths to address their weaknesses. When we have no idea what their strengths are, we have no obvious direction in which to turn to encourage improvement.

Jill also uses portfolios to help her students prepare for graduation, and she shares some management tips in the section below.

Preparing for Portfolios As a Graduation Requirement

Children spend many of their waking hours in school. In our schools, children make friends, develop passions, take on

Conference Goals

Student: **Grade:**   **Date:**

Present at conference:
Teachers:

Parent/guardians:

Other:

Portfolio Work Observations:

GOALS	The student will...	The family will...	The teachers will...

Additional notes, reminders, and/or suggestions:

Figure 6–2: *Conference Goal Sheet (developed by Jill Harrison Berg)*

challenges, love, hate, fight, eat, and even sleep when they need to. When it is time to move on from a school, to graduate and leave a school community, the occasion calls for a rite of passage. We like to celebrate, but this kind of juncture is also an essential time for reflection.

So the student is moving on to high school. Is he ready? Has she gotten what she should have out of this learning setting? Is he prepared for the challenges of the next phase in his learning? School administrators, teachers, parents, and students all benefit from accountability at these crucial junctures.

A student's demonstration of quality work, as the foundation of authentic assessment, should be the basis for his graduation. At the Cambridgeport School, students must prove that they are ready to graduate by completing a quality project in each major academic area which demonstrates the best of what they know and are able to do. They present these projects in front of a panel, composed of a variety of educational stakeholders (parents and other family members; community partners; former, current, and future teachers; and so on) who judge the presentation of the work using a rubric with which students are very familiar (see Figure 6–3).

The presentation helps all stakeholders, especially the student, feel confident in the student's worthiness to graduate. Portfolio projects are structured rigidly to hold students accountable for certain skills or standards in each subject area, but they are defined with a degree of latitude to allow students to exhibit their strengths and interests in a way that suits them.

The presentations have a visual as well as an oral and written component to accommodate students' individual presentation styles. Students who know themselves as learners can make choices that support their strengths and develop their weaknesses. Students, for example, can do their math project on any topic that contains the math concepts; they can bring in their knowledge and interest in dance, or animals, or computers. While developing their autobiography projects for English,

	How it looks **Aesthetics**	How you talk **Oral Communication**	How you write **Written Communication**
Student: **Panelist:**	Neatness Organization Adornment Clarity Care taken	Clear, loud voice Eye contact Appropriate word usage Decisiveness Engaging	Grammer/ punctuation Spelling Paragraphing and flow Word choice/ phrasing Style/voice
Math *Project*	Novice Apprentice Practitioner Expert	Novice Apprentice Practitioner Expert	Novice Apprentice Practitioner Expert
Comments			
Science *Project*	Novice Apprentice Practitioner Expert	Novice Apprentice Practitioner Expert	Novice Apprentice Practitioner Expert
Comments			
Research *Project*	Novice Apprentice Practitioner Expert	Novice Apprentice Practitioner Expert	Novice Apprentice Practitioner Expert
Comments			
Auto- *biography*	Novice Apprentice Practitioner Expert	Novice Apprentice Practitioner Expert	Novice Apprentice Practitioner Expert
Comments			

Figure 6–3: *Graduation Rubric (developed by the faculty of the Cambridgeport School)*

Thinking about work	Specialness	What it's all about
Reflection	**Creativity / Originality**	**Content**
Relevence	Takes chances	Detail
Personal growth	Unique approach	Complexity
Connections	Goes beyond	Accuracy
Empathy	Original work	Intraconnections
Change in thought	Personal stamp	Informative

Novice Apprentice Practitioner Expert	Novice Apprentice Practitioner Expert	Novice Apprentice Practitioner Expert

_____

_____

_____

Novice Apprentice Practitioner Expert	Novice Apprentice Practitioner Expert	Novice Apprentice Practitioner Expert

_____

_____

_____

Novice Apprentice Practitioner Expert	Novice Apprentice Practitioner Expert	Novice Apprentice Practitioner Expert

_____

_____

_____

Novice Apprentice Practitioner Expert	Novice Apprentice Practitioner Expert	Novice Apprentice Practitioner Expert

_____

_____

_____

students are offered opportunities to demonstrate their competence in many different forms of writing. And while preparing their projects for presentation, students are taught to use index cards, outlines, or even PowerPoint and/or other presentation aids, so that they can experiment and discover the tools that will help them to best communicate about their work to others.

A Manageable Portfolio System for Middle-School Teachers

Many teachers attempt to implement portfolio practices in their classrooms, only to find that halfway through the year they have piles of work so deep that the task of sorting through it is formidable. The keys to efficient portfolio use are having a routine and having the right materials. The Traveling Portfolio process should happen five or six times a year, but because Jill has a routine, by the second or third time she simply needs to tell her students, "It's Traveling Portfolio week," and the students know what that means. In fact, Traveling Portfolio weeks feel like a break for Jill because she needs to do a lot less teaching and preparation. The kids are engaged in the self-directed activities of collecting, selecting, and reflecting on their work. In order to begin, Jill recommends the tips and strategies in the box below.

Tips for Getting Started

1. Connect with colleagues on your team.
2. Be sure all participants are clear about your main objectives for using portfolios.
3. Obtain the proper organizational materials: folders, bins, files, binders, and so on.
4. Create a routine that students can fall into; schedule times to select and reflect.
5. Schedule portfolio development weeks in advance and stick to the dates.

Specific Strategies for Managing Portfolios

Many of the skills for collecting, selecting, and reflecting on student work begin in the earlier grades. Teachers throughout the school can support the portfolio development process, which will help build a learning culture.

- **Collect Student Work in a Binder**

  It is important to have a way to store passed-back work in the classroom. You can't simply tell students to clean out their desks and look for something to go in their portfolios. If work that you pass back gets lost in their bookbags or desks, it won't be available or neat enough to be used in the portfolio. I use three-ring binders, which are stored on a shelf in my classroom that students can reach. Each week or two when I pass back work the students have done, I ask students to take time to look at my comments and then file it in their binders. It will be there when we need it for portfolio week. The folders or binders must have enough space for at least one semester's work. To determine the size of the folders, you will need to decide if you will archive separately for each subject or collectively.

- **Date the Student Work and Build This into Assignments**

  Another important factor is that all work students do should be dated. When students are reflecting on their work and looking for changes over time, it is important that they have the data they need. You can assist them in this by always including a date line on teacher-created materials or keeping a date stamp in the room.

- **Create a Common Reflection Sheet: Produce Work Tags in Quantity**

  Streamlining the reflection process was not an easy task. I needed a Portfolio Work Tag, which was applicable to all kinds of work in all subjects. I didn't want to have a different one for the math teacher across the hall and a different one for the Spanish teacher, so I created a universal template around the principle that reflection requires one to look backward, inward, outward, and forward. I make up several hundred copies of the work tags at a time and kids know where they are kept in the classroom so that when they need one, they just go get it for themselves; it's self-directed.

- **Teach Students to Create Effective Cover Letters**
  The routine of writing the cover letter is something students become accustomed to as well. At the beginning of the year I assist students by providing an outline with the necessary information, but by the third round of portfolios, students generally do not need it. If I give them the date on which the portfolio is due back, they are able to write their own personal cover letters that use nicknames and families' jargon that endears their family members and invites a thoughtful response.

  Personalizing the cover letters is important because every family has its own unique relationship and the cover letter is the key to opening the communication with the parents. You want real dialogue to happen and not just a situation where the parents are signing off on something; helping kids to find ways to make it personal helps a lot because every parent appreciates getting love letters from their children.

- **Schedule Portfolio Weeks Around Grading and Conference Dates**
  I recommend taking time at the beginning of the school year to schedule the portfolio weeks. They often fall into place quite logically as you plan them to coincide with conferences and report cards. For example, we know that our parent conferences are going to be in mid-November, and we know that we want to have a portfolio week between September and then. Introducing portfolios to kids as something they are going to do regularly helps to establish the rhythm of it, the regularity of it, and helps to make it manageable.

- **Use Sturdy Portfolio Folders That Make the Work Special**

  The portfolio folders themselves need to be something that honors the work inside them. They need to be carefully created by the student or purchased and personalized so that each student feels that his folder is special. I further develop the mystique by asking students to wash their hands before handling them or by refusing to let them take them home when it is raining. The folders need to be sturdy but also large and thick enough to accommodate the work they are likely to take home (larger than 8½ x 11 and thick enough for a videotape or homemade book, for example).

- **Videotaping Requires the Right Materials**

  Videotapes are an effective way to document accomplishment in a variety of intelligences; however, they can be a large headache for the teacher. Individual classroom performances can easily be taped if each student is assigned his or her own portfolio tape. Tape each performance directly onto the student's portfolio tape; do not make a master and then condemn yourself to dubbing them onto individual tapes.

  Group performances are more difficult. When a group of my students wrote and produced a play, I videotaped it. I wanted to dub it onto each of their portfolio tapes so they could take it home. I found that the only realistic way to do this without spending all of my free time for a week was to find a dubbing machine.

  In another instance, student pairs made history presentations. I taped all of them, but I taped them with the school camera, which uses expensive miniature tapes. Due to the cost of the tapes, each teacher was only given one, so I had to make sure to make the time to copy the presentations off it before the tape filled up, so that I could use the same tape again from the beginning for more presentations. That was a management nightmare. It is well worth it to invest in the right materials: enough tapes, a dubbing machine, a portfolio tape for each student, etc.

- **Create a Portfolio-Return System and Filing Procedure**

  Certain materials make the portfolio-return system easier, too. When portfolio folders are returned, students can turn them in on their own if you designate a box (I use an old trunk, my colleague uses a fish tank) and provide a clipboard where students can check off their own names. I later go through the folders to remove the contents, and to check on parent responses. When all portfolios have been returned, I take the work out of them, put a big paper clip on the whole packet, and file it in our classroom archive, a large hanging file folder box. I have a hanging file for each student and the work is filed directly behind his or her name.

  At the end of the school year when preparing for Portfolio Day, instead of sorting through 180 days' worth of work, my students have a culled selection of work that they have already reflected on and can use for their exhibition. Students can always access the binders if there is some other outstanding work that they did or something they really enjoyed that they want to include to present a more well-rounded view of themselves as a learner.

The Power of Traveling Portfolios for Adolescents

Jill's insights over the course of the year tell a great deal about how powerful Traveling Portfolios have become for students, teachers, and parents from her classroom community. By documenting growth and achievement, the portfolio describes each student's journey as a learner for that year. As eighth-grade students end their middle-school career, their conference and graduation presentations remain a vivid example of accomplishment. As Jill so poignantly describes:

At the end of the year, the collection of archived work from the year's Traveling Portfolios represents quite an achievement. In our school, students cull the work in this archive and prepare a smaller selection of work to present at our school's annual Portfolio Day and to include in their permanent portfolios.

Although Portfolio Day is primarily a day of celebration, it is also a day of learning for us all—parents, teachers, and students. We learn how far we have come in one short school year by working together and thinking critically about student work.

Students themselves see their strengths; they set goals to meet their areas of challenge. Their reflective work tells the story of how students' portfolios help them set goals for improvement and truthfully and respectfully take ownership of their learning.

One student reflected on his Portfolio Work Tag, "All the time when I type something I tend to say things that people may not understand. I want to work on making something clear."

Another reflected, "I think [this work] shows how much I love sports and how much better I can do on things if it's about something I enjoy like sports. I think I would do better if I took it slower and read the article more carefully."

Traveling Portfolios are windows for all in the community to see how students are learning. As Jill so appropriately summarizes:

Adolescents feel a tremendous sense of power from this Traveling Portfolio system, which helps them to demonstrate that they can recognize areas for improvement, make a plan to improve these areas, and achieve improvement before a community that cares about them.

Chapter 7

Organizing and Sustaining a Learning Culture
Lynn F. Stuart

Making learning rigorous and joyful in all the ways human beings learn, making learning visible, making learning public are what a good education is all about. None of these ideals is possible in the absence of a professional community of teachers who work and study together in order to teach our children well.

(Lynn F. Stuart and Evangeline Harris Stefanakis)

A focus on learning and teaching in a climate that prizes working together has always been an overriding goal for the Cambridgeport School. This goal has helped us think about how adults model working collaboratively, how children learn individually and in groups, how families share in learning, and how we develop a common language to talk about learning. As a principal, I believe that one of my most essential responsibilities is to expand conversations about how children learn, what they know, and what they can do. Collectively, we ask how we can deepen our understanding of the knowledge base of teaching.

Together the faculty and I have been asking questions about what is important in learning and teaching. Since time is a kind of gatekeeper for action, our first task has always been to find time to meet, to work together, and to answer our questions. Second, we have needed to structure the time we have together. Third, we have needed to protect our time together so that other demands do not keep us from asking both big and practical questions.

Creating Opportunities for Structured Conversations About Learning and Teaching

Over the course of our first ten years, we have come to value and protect several kinds of faculty collaboration. At the heart of our goal which is to better understand our students, their learning, and our teaching is the notion of what I call *structured conversations*. Our first efforts focused on children and their work and were guided by the protocol for a "Staff Review of a Child" that was developed by Patricia Carini (1982). Then in 1995, we had the good fortune to work with Harvard University's Project Zero and the Massachusetts Department of Education in a grant that would help focus our conversations about learning further. Several other kinds of conversations emerged through our work with Project Zero and the Department of Education; which centered on *Key Practices* (Seidel 1997).

Embedded into the Key Practices is a strong intellectual commitment to explore and affirm ideas, processes, and products of learning. As our Key Practices conversations moved

---

Five Key Portfolio Practices

- **Collaborative Assessment:** Conversations about children's work

- **Classroom Practices:** Conversations about using projects & portfolios as curriculum and assessment

- **Language and Ideas:** Conversations about the language and ideas of portfolio assessment

- **Communicating with the Community:** Conversations with all members of school about the new approaches to assessment

- **Celebrating Student Work:** Conversations with children to publicly celebrate their products

---

(Adapted from Seidel 1997)

more purposefully into the fabric of our school culture, we developed new structures and borrowed others. Our Staff Review of Curriculum blended formats adapted from Expeditionary Learning Schools and the Coalition of Essential Schools. Our Peer Consultancy was derived from these sources and our own need to have short, focused conversations about a challenge a teacher was facing. It is not uncommon to observe one of a collection of protocols in action at a staff meeting.

Perhaps the most important structures for ongoing collaboration are the large- and small-group meetings (grade-level team meetings, cluster meetings, mixed small-group meetings, and the whole-faculty meeting). A second more in-depth practice has been our annual summer workshop at which the entire faculty meets to consider topics we have defined. These topics always revolve around curriculum and assessment. It was at a summer workshop where we devised our two-year curriculum cycles, where we first explored rubrics, where we debated a grading system for the upper grades, and where we struggled with identifying *essential performances* of learning. An offshoot of the summer workshop has been the mid-winter retreat—an afternoon meeting from 1 to 6 P.M. with a dinner following.

Structures for Talking About Learning

- Faculty Meetings (Whole Group)
- All-Faculty Summer Workshop and Mid-Winter Retreat
- Team Meetings/Cluster Meetings (grade level, cross-grade)
- Small-Group Meetings (90-minute occasional meetings)
- Peer Triads (observations and debriefing sessions)
- Workshops, Courses, and Conferences (occasional)
- Alternative Professional Time (3 hours weekly for 12-week periods)

There are also occasional structured one-and-a-half-hour meetings during school time when half the faculty comes together to discuss a topic (while their colleagues, student teachers, and instructional assistants are in charge of the classrooms). The groups then switch with a second hour and a half being devoted to discussion with the rest of the faculty. These discussions are important, for they represent a way for professional teachers, student teachers, and paraprofessionals to all come to the table together. Topics include student reflections, organizing the end-of-year portfolios, documentation of group learning, and project-based learning that capitalizes on multiple intelligences.

Alternative Professional Time: A Focus on Teachers As Researchers

A second structure for conversations and study about learning and teaching is what we call Alternative Professional Time, often referred to as AP Time[1]. AP Time is time carved out of the school day for professional development and teacher research. Conceptualized as an opportunity for teachers to seek professional development of their own choice, it began as more of an individual endeavor. Over the years the need for collective support for AP Time work and the desire to work in groups led to teams of teachers working together on a project or in discussions.

AP Time is defined as up to three hours, one day per week, for twelve weeks. During this period student teachers are well grounded in the practice of their assigned classroom. Thus, the student teacher and/or assistant teacher is able to take over the class while the teacher is at work in the school or at another location. There is a deep belief in the importance and power of teachers designing professional development that

---

[1]Based on a model developed at the Devotion School in Brookline, MA by a small group of teachers, we asked ourselves if all teachers and specialists in our school might benefit from AP Time.

meets their needs and a concomitant trust in their work. There is also a requirement from the outset that AP Time should never detract from student learning.[2]

How have the teachers used AP Time? Memorable AP Time projects have included Jill Berg's development of a Traveling Portfolio process for upper-grade students. Like a number of individual or group projects, this project was shared with colleagues. Traveling Portfolios are now a regular part of the home–school communication for upper-grade students and their families, as you have discovered in the story of Jill's classroom in the previous chapter. Two other AP Time projects have had wide impact on the school. One was a third/fourth-grade study of the fourth-grade MCAS questions and student responses in math. Guided by a colleague/critical friend from Wheelock College, where we have participated in a Professional Development School partnership, this three-person teaching team studied the test. More importantly, they also looked thoughtfully at individual children, the curriculum, and the ways they teach.

Another AP Time study was conducted as part of a research collaboration with Tufts University professors and grade 1/2 teachers who were eager to look at children's language development at home and in school. They tried to discern ways to make the culture of the home and the school respectful partners in learning. This study was one of several reasons that the whole faculty chose to deepen our study of issues of race, class, and language differences as they affect our teaching. AP Time is a key reminder of the value of professional study and engagement in the ideas, research, and reflective practices of teaching.

Yet another vehicle for working together is the organization of classroom practice groups. These groups include *peer triads* in

---

[2]The classes, led ably by student teachers who were ready to get their feet wet, carried on their regular learning routines. An important factor is that AP Time requires no cost to the school or district. AP Time needs to be protected each year, for it is a difficult thing to make arrangements to leave one's class for a period of time (usually 7–9 weeks in the fall and again during the spring semester).

which three teachers who do not teach at the same grade level are teamed for focused observations of each other's teaching. These observations are followed by a debriefing session when notes, ideas, and suggestions are shared. We also use a protocol called a *Peer Consultancy* in which teachers gather in small groups for fifteen minutes at the start of a faculty meeting and address a specific issue that one member of the group has brought. This format is designed to provide a quick response to a problem or idea that a teacher wants to discuss with colleagues. Colleagues listen for five minutes, ask clarifying questions, and then fire off some ideas for the presenting teacher to think about later.

These school-based structures for professional development are augmented by courses (sometimes we have chosen to take a single course together) or workshops, conferences, and individual study that are later shared in small- or large-group settings. Each of these formats for collaborative work has the potential to create and sustain meaningful conversations about teaching and learning. But each brings organizational challenges to us as well.

Challenges and Opportunities: Serving Diverse Learners in a Whole-School Community

High standards for meaningful learning in an environment that respects and utilizes multiple intelligences in teaching and assessment are essential to a good school. Also essential are the careful observation and documentation of student work that reveals the strengths and needs of each learner. We cannot erase all differences among learners. Such differences challenge us to find new ways to teach all students. Indeed, differences enrich a world where they are respected. We must remain steadfast in helping everyone get smarter and in leaving no one behind. It takes nothing less than a whole-school effort to reach this goal.

The teachers and students tell the story of learning better than a principal ever could, but leadership is vital. It takes a laserlike focus on learning, teaching, and assessment in the midst of a sea of organizational complexities. It is the principal's job to protect the values held by a school. It is the principal's job to be the *principal learner* in the school, setting an example of inquiry into learning as well as establishing the structures that make inquiry possible. It is the principal's job to celebrate the many ways both teachers and students learn. It is everybody's job to communicate these goals to the wider school community and to the public.

Chapter 8

Multiple Intelligences and Portfolios As a Window into Learners' Minds: Key Lessons Learned

Multiple entry places for multiple ways of knowing and acting in the world mean that we can no longer dare to measure learning in a singular way. We must always respect the power of language (oral and written in many different tongues) as an essential human skill in both technical terms and in expressive terms. Language and dance, math and music, archeology and architecture, science and the arts—these "languages" express in myriad ways the human condition and the universe of ideas and possibilities. Portfolios capture the fullness of this experience.

(Evangeline Harris Stefanakis and Lynn F. Stuart)

Chapter 7 concluded this story of implementing MI theory and portfolios, with Lynn Stuart retelling her community's journey in developing and sustaining a collaborative learning culture. This background set a context for better understanding how Bela, Sarah, and Jill created their portfolio classrooms over a period of several years. Lynn's journey into school change was unique as she was a leader who nurtured a learning environment based on MI theory and portfolios. Lynn explains how she started:

Starting and ending places are always lonely if approached alone! The notion of sitting beside the learner, sitting beside one's colleagues, sitting beside the families we serve is the powerful connector that allows human learning to become visible through multiple perspectives that are shared in portfolios.

In this chapter, I offer a series of lessons learned about multiple intelligences theory and portfolios through my own work with Cambridgeport and other schools. I suggest an assessment framework that is compatible with the push for greater accountability and standards-based reform. Like Howard Gardner and others who study assessment, I advocate for a comprehensive assessment system to more completely report on student learning over time, not a single set of tests. I summarize key lessons learned from experienced teachers and offer the Key Practices as a road map for practitioners to adapt in order to sustain a whole-school or classroom portfolio culture.

It Begins with a Clear Vision and Belief in Multiple Intelligences as a Community

In our preparation for writing, I asked Lynn why a book about MI theory and portfolios needs to be written. We agreed that in the wake of current school reform we observe that the concrete focus on the individual differences in students as learners is getting lost. As Lynn suggested:

> Being smart, understanding how one learns at home, at school, or in the world, growing smarter—these are topics that raise important questions for learners of all ages. "Smart" is too frequently the concept that divides us, that opens or closes doors, or that places us on a ladder where we are either destined to go up, teeter in the middle, or have a difficult time at or near the bottom. So, what is "smart" and how do we nurture a culture of smartness in our schools?

In Chapters 1 and 2, I suggest key ideas on how to apply the theory of multiple intelligences. Building on Gardner's MI theory, I agree that *being smart* is multifaceted; it is not a singular quality. The greatest challenge of educators today is to understand the complexity of the multiple intelligences that each student brings to school, but may not use (as the Poor Learner recounts in Chapter 1). Similarly, each teacher brings a unique MI profile that needs to be understood, along with an array of approaches to learning and teaching. The larger challenge remains: how does a whole community learn to observe, to understand, and to nurture each individual student's learning? How *do* schools and individual educators strive to teach all students and sustain themselves in this hard work?

Shifting both philosophy and pedagogy to apply MI theory to classroom practices raises dilemmas for a school community. It requires a new way of viewing high standards in an environment which values individual differences. We are learning to seek standards, not standardization. We create multiple ways of teaching and learning that personalize the process and honor the learner's needs and strengths. Teaching and learning take on new dimensions. We, as educators, move from teacher to coach, from isolated activities to real-world, project-based tasks, teaching across traditional subject domains. We move from classrooms that were filling stations to places where complex problems are uncovered, solved, and discovered anew.

Why Consider the Whole School?

- Schools are organisms- all parts must share beliefs

- Children learn the values and practices of the whole school as a learning community

- Student progress is the concern of students, teachers, parents, and the educational community

- Each school is a unique learning community which adds a context to student work

Individual Differences Are Celebrated in Theory and Practice in a Whole School

The Cambridgeport School, like many urban and rural schools, must educate a diverse population. It has become a place where individual learning differences are celebrated and nurtured. From the beginning, as Lynn notes in Chapter 4, the Cambridgeport community decided to value multiple ways of learning and multiple ways of documenting learning. With research and researchers, like myself and others, to support them, the school built a culture where the entire community would actively learn together. As Lynn and her teachers recounted:

> The community decided to broaden their lens for understanding learning and the culture in which it can prosper. And prosper it will, if we only sit beside each other, observing closely, posing difficult questions, challenging ourselves and our students to stretch beyond the standard and the known, and integrating assessment of the learning into our daily lives.

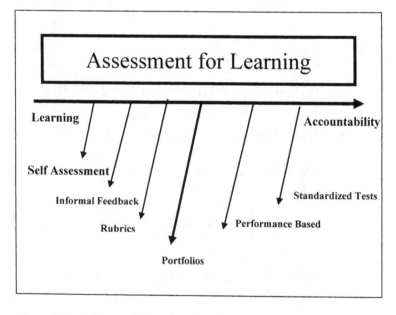

Figure 8–1: *Assessment for Learning Continuum*

Building a Comprehensive Assessment System

The drive toward standardized and state testing requires us, as researchers and practitioners, to find ways to learn from tests *and* portfolios in order to develop a comprehensive assessment system in which accountability would be demonstrated at many levels related to student achievement. In Chapter 4, Lynn graphically portrayed a comprehensive system within the Cambridge Public Schools. In a more generalized way, I offer a design for a comprehensive system which combines formal, informal, and classroom assessments, including portfolios, to inform the state, the district, the school, and the teacher. The goal for each district is to carefully construct a comprehensive assessment system, with a collection of assessments that allow many stakeholders to use these data to improve both student learning and teachers' teaching. Without portfolios to make visible what students do and what teachers teach, I am not sure this can be done. Figure 8–1 presents my representation for an assessment for learning continuum.

Building a Culture for Change: Key Practices and Structured Learning Conversations

How does portfolio assessment and curriculum based on multiple intelligences theory take root in schools? Simply, there is no one way to do this. Themes and patterns have emerged from pioneer efforts in different settings. From 1994 to 1997, with colleagues from Harvard Project Zero (PZ) and the Massachusetts Department of Education, I worked with schools across the state to implement project-based learning and portfolio assessment in line with Standards-Based Reform and the new State Curriculum Frameworks. As co-director of this project with my colleague Steve Seidel, I traveled four days a week to five schools (we eventually added eight more schools in year two and three). Repeatedly, we saw the power of portfolios and the importance of looking at student work to actively engage a whole-school community in changing their classroom practices to better teach their diverse learners. We purposely worked in challenging urban and rural environments and struggled to collaboratively learn *with* these communities, as a team of researchers, leaders, teachers, parents, and children. Collectively, we were regularly sitting beside each other to look at student work.

A set of Key Practices guided our work in each school. Adopting the Key Practices provided a vital framework to help a whole school focus reform efforts on the students and their learning, avoiding the distractions of many initiatives. As the schema in Figure 8–2 shows, student work and student learning became the central focus for the community, and celebrating student work is key.

The Key Practices as structured conversations provided time for faculties to look at student work from portfolios. The teachers' goal in these conversations was to collectively think about how their students are learning and how effectively they are teaching. Different schools adapted the Key Practices in

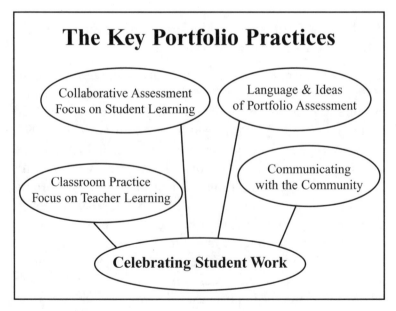

Figure 8–2: *Key Practices*

ways that fit their schedules, using staff meetings, common planning time, and after-school sessions to drive the reform efforts. These practices require that each teacher engage in focused and individualized professional development, using students' work as data to improve their daily classroom practice. ATLAS Communities (another reform model) has adopted a modified version of these Key Practices. In the ATLAS model, teacher study groups collaboratively look at student work and achievement data to drive changes related to teaching all students. The quality of schooling is evident in the quality of its students' work. As Lynn F. Stuart and I collaboratively discovered:

> Two students sharing work, a group of teachers analyzing a student project, a teacher and a principal conferencing about a science experiment just observed, an administrator and a researcher connecting practice and theory—these are examples of how "sitting beside" is the vehicle for learning about learning. Sitting beside each other is the place to start; sitting beside each other is the place to continue as a whole school community reaches for achievement in many arenas. Sitting beside each other is the place we preserve to celebrate each individual's accomplishment and competence.

Reflection As the Key to Maintaining a Learning Culture

In Chapters 3, 5, and 6, I describe teachers' classroom practices related to guiding their students in reflecting, focusing initially on Bela, then on Sarah and Jill. Collection, selection, and reflection in each of the classrooms define a set of common portfolio practices graphically portrayed in Chapter 2. These schoolwide portfolio practices define a developmental framework that ensures examining student work at every grade level. Teachers develop reflective protocols for student self-assessment to fit their learners' developmental level. Reflection on student work is what all the learners in the community do, adults and children, to *get better* at learning.

As Lynn described in Chapter 4:

> One of the critical elements of any system of assessment is feed-back—the continuous loop of response to and reflection on student thinking and work in progress.

> From our school's experience, I believe that the greatest power in using portfolios resides in the personalization of assessment through the descriptive processes that capture thinking and performance at many stages.

Personalization, I agree, is vital to engaging all learners, but it is not sufficient to understand how to best assess and teach all students. It is important to know each student, but it is equally important to know how that student is doing in meeting a set of criteria or standards. Individually *and* collectively a school community sets goals for continuous improvement in a data-driven school reform era.

Rubrics are helpful because they establish specific criteria for assessment and create clarity about standards set at many levels—by the state, by the school, by the classroom community, for an assignment. Rubrics, acting as an assessment accordion, can guide teachers and students to reflect on understanding, on performance related to standards, on personal goals, and on individual progress. Rubrics help a school knit together accountability and assessment for learning purposes, simultaneously looking at the student and the system's needs.

Meeting Rigorous Standards Using Rubrics in a Learning Community

As Jill reminds us in Chapter 6, school standards become public in scoring rubrics for portfolios and for eighth-grade graduation. Cambridgeport School requires eighth-grade students to engage in long-term projects in the major subject areas—English/Language Arts, social studies, math, and science. Eighth graders are also required to develop organizational and "executive function" skills of increasingly independent work complete with an accountability system built into their scoring rubrics. These rubrics and the portfolio presentations have created a culture of high standards and simultaneously offer a way for individual students to get meaningful and rigorous feedback about their learning from parents, teachers, and community members.

Sustaining a Learning Culture: Portfolio Rituals and Traditions of Celebration

Curriculum exhibitions and Portfolio Celebration Days become cherished rituals in schools where students' and teachers' work is publicly celebrated. Adults enjoy students' presentations and performances. Each individual's growth, as evidenced in a portfolio, is made visible to families and the wider community. At other times, exhibitions of student work may be as simple or as elaborate as those Sarah described in Chapter 5—the "museum" tours of the artifacts and written diaries created by students during their study of the American Revolution.

In Chapter 2, we considered how to celebrate student work by compiling the end-of-the-year or pass-along portfolio. The portfolio is evidence of growth, a measure of learning, and a chronicle of the classroom journey of both teacher and student because of their joint collection, selection, and reflection process. It becomes more than just individual pieces of work— a portfolio is a collective product of student learning!

Portfolio Celebration Day at the Cambridgeport School allows families and visitors to look at portfolios and celebrate student learning by reviewing students' work. Portfolio visitors are given the following reflective questions to ask children as they visit classrooms throughout the school.

Portfolio Celebration Reflection

1. How was this piece done?
2. What do you like best about this piece of work?
3. If you did it again, what would you change?
4. What did you learn from doing this work?

The Portfolio Celebration Folder for Parents is available on the CD-ROM.

To "knit" the school and teachers' stories together, the following summarizes a collection of Community Based Portfolio Lessons:

I. Creating a Learning Culture in the Whole School Comes with a Clarity of Vision

- MI as a theory embodied in a learning community (see Chapter 1).
- All students are smart in different ways is a belief system (see Chapter 1).
- A community combines high standards *and* learning and teaching diversity.
- A professional community talks about what is possible for all adults and all children.

II. Becoming a School That Teaches Diverse Learners Using Multiple Intelligences

- Portfolios of student work become evidence that all students learn in different ways.
- Leaders, teachers, parents use portfolios to see the diverse capabilities of all learners.
- Portfolios become the learners' footprints—student work is evidence and learning data.

III. Documenting Learning with a Portfolio for Every Student Across the Grades

- Start to implement portfolios slowly: SSS means Start Slow and Small (see Chapters 2, 3).
- Just collect student work to begin (see Chapters 1 and 2).
- Select an array of work using MI as an analytic tool (see Chapter 2).
- Select work as evidence of growth and diverse

---

capabilities (see Chapters 3, 4, and 5).
- Reflect on student work and on the learning process (see Chapters 3, 4, 5, and 6).
- Compile and manage student work in reasonable ways (see Chapters 3, 5, and 6).

IV.   Developing and Adapting a Framework and Support for Portfolios

- Develop a culture of structured conversations focused on learning (see Chapter 8).
- Consider a set of Key Practices for multiple audiences (see Chapter 7).
- Document and celebrate portfolios and projects (see Chapter 4).
- Design and develop exhibitions and project-based learning (see Chapter 4).

The Teachers' Stories: Lessons Learned from Educators using MI and Portfolios

Bela Bhasin, Sarah Fiarman, Jill Harrison Berg, and others explain how they understand the multiple intelligences of their students by examining individual student work. Each teacher uses student work to create MI profiles and portfolios to observe, to keep track of, and to document individual students' learning. Profiles and portfolios help teachers, at different grade levels, adapt their teaching to meet individual needs, customizing their practices to respond to the developmental level of their students. Simply, there is no one way to "do portfolios." The beauty of portfolios is that they adapt to the context of the community, the school, the classroom, and the child.

Surprisingly, although Bela, Sarah, and Jill apply MI theory and use portfolios differently to create a learning culture in their classrooms, they have a common set of practices—a set of three Ps that emerge as recurring themes.

1. **Personalize** the assessment process with portfolios.
   - Use portfolios to create MI profiles of individual learners' strengths.
   - Assess students by sitting beside the learner regularly with the student's work.
   - Look at student work; listen to what students say about their work.
   - Help students reflect on what they do, how they do it, and what they learn.
   - Look at student work to see who the child is as a linguist, scientist, mathematician, cooperative learner, and as a reflective learner.

2. **Pluralize** the curriculum with multiple entry points.
   - Redesign curriculum using MI as a framework and the interests of students and teachers.
   - Use MI as a lens to assess the classroom environment.
   - Pluralize activities using all intelligences—in art, music, kinesthetic, interpersonal, and interpersonal activities.
   - Ensure that portfolio contents reflect evidence of the student's MI profile.

3. **Problem solve** about how to best assess and teach all students using student work.

   - Problem solve using conversations about student work as outlined in Chapters 3, 4, and 7.
   - Problem solve using student work as a guide to understand students with bilingual or special educational needs and adapt curriculum and assessments accordingly.

Each of these teachers agrees that collaborative assessment, looking at student work, and asking questions allows them to build an inclusive classroom that can accommodate a wide range of learning needs.

Epilogue: Lessons in Education

The teachers portrayed in this book revised their portfolio practices using MI theory as an analytic tool to assess their environment, to assess their students' work, and to assess their own classroom practices. How do members of a school community see MI and portfolios as a window into the learner's mind?

In a piece titled "Lessons in Education," Derrick Jackson, a political columnist for the *Boston Globe*, asks fundamental questions about how schools define intelligence or smartness in relation to the testing mania that consumes Massachusetts and the United States (Jackson 2001). Jackson, like Howard Gardner, suggests that a lingering single view of intelligence, and the subsequent single focus on passing a standardized test that has high stakes, favors those students who have strong linguistic and mathematical skills. Only a small percentage of students in diverse populations have the defined English language skills and academic vocabulary to score well even though they may have adequate linguistic intelligence. What happens if tests alone are used to tell the story of the diverse learners in today's schools?

Derrick Jackson suggests that powerful learning for all children is visible in portfolios and exhibitions, which he states are more valuable than any test. Seeing how each individual is smart, not who is smart in test performance, is the lesson of education that seems to be forgotten. As he writes:

> In April, U.S. Education Secretary Rod Paige defended the test craze . . . tests give each child an identity. That has stuck with me for two months because if he wanted to see identity, he could have come to my 10-year-old's school. That same month the 5/6 grade of the Cambridgeport School . . . . put on what they call their Living Wax Museum. In a huge history project, 68 students selected a figure from the 1700s or 1800s. They read several

books about the figure and then wrote autobiographies that in some cases were twenty pages long. They made costumes to assume that figure's role in a school assembly.

Paige often says that tests are the way to find if schools are failing. The Living Wax Museum allowed families to build toward a great day of success.

Most important, these 10-, 11-, and 12-year-olds had to do tremendous amounts of critical thinking. Students had to think about the historical context of their figures. They were encouraged to pick figures who were different from them in race, color and gender. Many children did.

MI-based projects *personalize* learning, *pluralize* the curriculum and assessments, and set high standards for diverse learners. As Jackson describes:

> On Living Wax day, the cauldron of preparation bubbled onto the auditorium floor. The love of learning streamed out from under the wigs, headdresses, and hats . . . virtually all the children were bursting with pride and information that many parents did not know.

> What you discovered were students who had learned far more about singular reasons a person is remembered in history (i.e., multiple choice test reasons). The students learned that all of their biographical subjects achieved greatness because they struggled with doubt, climbed over societal barriers, or placed morality and principle above popularity.

As a journalist, Jackson could see that MI and portfolios offer a window into each learner's mind. He wrote:

> Meredith [in her portfolio reflection] wrote about why John Adams defended the British soldiers who show the civilian patriots in the Boston Massacre.

> In this child's words—*"No one would defend the soldiers in court, but when asked I agreed because, unlike most patriots, justice and fairness were more important to me than patriotism."*

> Molly (in her report and portfolio reflection) describes how she

learned how life was difficult for female astronomy pioneer Maria Mitchell.

In this child's words—*"In Rome, I looked forward to visiting the famous Vatican observatory but was angry and disappointed to hear that women were not allowed in. After several weeks, I got special permission to enter, but could only visit during the day so I could not view the stars. . . ."*

Nathaniel writes, in his reflection, about how Benjamin Bannaker turned insults into compliments: Thomas Jefferson had written uniformly that blacks are of inferior mental intelligence to whites . . . .

In this child's words—*"I was disgusted with this as I thought Thomas Jefferson to be a very great man and I sent him a copy of my almanac and a very polite note asking him to reconsider his biased opinions. Jefferson replied, he said he had not really meant what he had written. He had been extremely impressed with my almanac."*

Bannaker responded. . . . the color of the skin is unrelated to the powers of the mind or intellectual being.

These Cambridgeport students are actively learning in a school where MI and portfolios allow teachers and parents *to sit beside* learners to see their unique profiles. This culture allows teachers to become researchers of individuals, consistently looking for students' interests and strengths to build on. As Jackson so aptly reminds us:

> No standardized test nourishes the mind or intellect as do projects where one transports the body and mind back in time. Two months later, my son's teachers said that two boys who respectively played Frederick Douglas and John Brown are continuing to debate in class the merits of violence and non-violence in the struggle for freedom.

> These boys . . . have traveled back in time, the past is now . . . a part of them. The next generation of leaders is much more likely to come from children like Paul, Kelsey, Molly, or Nathaniel, who understand not just what people did, but how they came to do what they did.

> The *how* is almost never on a standardized test.

As Jackson suggests—*the how is never in a test*. It is both *what is learned* and *how it is learned* that is always in portfolios, and can always be retold.

As Emma, from Grade 5 reminds us, a portfolio can be a window into a learner's mind:

> We had to think of a way that our class was sort of like a metaphor. My classroom metaphor is in my work, in my piece of art . . . It is my drawing of a hand. I drew different wrinkles in the hand, because like the wrinkles, everyone in our class is unique.

I invite educators who value the diversity in the minds of today's learners to remember that multiple intelligences theory asks for multiple assessments. We cannot erase differences among learners (these differences challenge us to find new ways to teach all children), but we as educators can be steadfast in helping everyone get smarter, leaving no one behind. Multiple intelligences and portfolios can become windows into understanding learners' minds, their possibilities, and their competence!

A colleague of mine refers to efforts of change in all the messy and sometimes unpredictable ways that new ideas or new practices take root. It is important to support that "mucking about" in the explorations of teachers in blending knowledge about multiple ways of knowing and doing into their teaching practice and the life of their classrooms. Not unlike the "foreigner" in any land who listens, watches, and haltingly makes attempts at a new language, teachers are in some ways traveling on foreign soil as they seek to change their practice to reflect all the ways human beings learn and to assess learning in its fullness instead of through a narrow lens. We must give them support to learn the new "languages" of intelligence as well as teaching to and with multiple intelligences so that they may respond fluently and with confidence and competence.

References

Allen, D. 1998. *Assessing Student Learning: From Grading to Understanding*. New York: Teachers College Press.

Armstrong, T. [1994] 1999. *Multiple Intelligences for the Classroom*. Alexandria, VA: Association for Supervision and Curriculum Development.

Bailey, J. 2000. *Implementing Student Led Conferences*. Thousand Oaks, CA: Corwin Press.

Bellanca, J. 1997. *Multiple Assessments for Multiple Intelligences*. Arlington Heights, IL: IRI Skylight.

Bennett, R. E., and Ward, A. 1993. *Construction Versus Choice in Cognitive Measurement: Issues in Constructed Response, Performance Testing, and Portfolio Assessment*. Hillsdale, NJ: Erlbaum Associates.

Black, L. 1994. *New Directions in Portfolio Assessment: Reflective Practice, Critical Theory and Large-Scale Scoring*. Portsmouth, NH: Boynton/Cook.

Campbell, L., Campbell, B., and Dickinson, D. 1996. *Teaching and Learning Through Multiple Intelligences*. Needham, MA: Allyn and Bacon.

Campbell, L., and Campbell, B. 1999. *Multiple Intelligences and Student Achievement: Six Success Stories for Six Schools*. Alexandria, VA: Association for Supervision and Curriculum Development.

Carini, P. 1982. *The School Lives of Seven Children*. Grand Forks, ND: North Dakota Study Group on Evaluation.

Chapman, C. 1996. *Multiple Intelligences Centers and Projects*. Arlington Heights, IL: IRI Skylight Training and Publishers.

Commonwealth of Massachusetts, Department of Education, Education Reform Restructuring Network: Project Zero, 1995–97.

Darling-Hammond, L., and Ancess, J. 1994. *Graduation by Portfolio at Central Park East Secondary School.* New York: National Center for Restructuring Education, Schools and Teaching (NCREST).

Detterman, D. K. 1994. *Theories of Intelligence.* Norwood, NJ: Ablex.

Fogarty, R. 1995. *Integrating Curricula with Multiple Intelligences: Teams, Themes and Threads.* Palatine, IL: IRI Skylight.

———. 1997. *Problem-Based Learning and Other Curricula Models for the Multiple Intelligences Classroom.* Arlington Heights, IL: IRI Skylight Publishers.

Gardner, H. 1983, 1993. *Frames of Mind: The Theory of Multiple Intelligences.* New York: Basic Books.

———. 1991. *The Unschooled Mind: How Children Think and How Schools Should Teach.* New York: Basic Books.

———. 1993. *Multiple Intelligences: The Theory in Practice.* New York: Basic Books.

———. 1996. *Intelligence: Multiple Perspectives.* Fort Worth, TX: Harcourt Brace College Publishers.

———. 1999. *Intelligence Reframed: Multiple Intelligences for the 21st Century.* New York: Basic Books.

———. 1999. *The Disciplined Mind: What All Students Should Understand.* New York: Simon & Schuster.

Gardner, H., Kornhaber, M. L., and Wake, W. K. 1997. *Intelligence: Multiple Perspectives.* Florence, KY: International Thompson.

Gentile, C., et al. 1995. *Windows into the Classroom: NAEP's 1992 Writing Portfolio Study.* Washington, D.C.: Office of Education Research and Improvement, U.S. Department of Education.

Grosvenor, L. 1993. *Student Portfolios.* Washington, D.C.: NEA Professional Library.

Gutloff, K., ed. 1996. *Multiple Intelligences.* West Haven, CT: NEA Professional Library.

Himley, M. (ed.), with P. Carini. 2000. *From Another Angle: Children's Strengths and Schools Standards, The Prospect Center's Descriptive Review of the Child.* New York: Teachers College Press.

Hoerr, T. 2000. *Becoming a Multiple Intelligences School.* Alexandria, VA: Association for Supervision and Curriculum Development.

Holdaway, D. 1983. *Foundations of Literacy,* New York: Scholastic.

Jackson, D. 2001. "Lessons in Education." *Boston Globe* (6 June).

Knight, M., et al. 1994. *Portfolio Assessment: Applications of Portfolio Analysis.* Landham, MD: University Press of America.

———. 1999. *Eight Ways of Knowing: Teaching for Multiple Intelligence:* Palatine, IL: IRI Skylight.

Kornhaber, M. 1994. *The Theory of Multiple Intelligences: Why and How Schools Use It: A Pilot Study.* Unpublished qualifying paper, Harvard Graduate School of Education, Cambridge, MA.

———. 1994. *Seeking Strengths: Equitable Identification for Gifted Education and the Theory of Multiple Intelligence.* Unpublished doctoral thesis. Harvard Graduate School of Education, Cambridge, MA.

Lazear, D. G. 1994. *Multiple Intelligence Approaches to Assessment: Solving the Assessment Conundrum.* Tucson, AZ: Zephyr Press.

———. 2000. *Pathways of Learning: Teaching Students and Parents About Multiple Intelligences.* Tucson, AZ: Zephyr Press.

Little, J. W. 1982. "Norms of Collegiality and Experimentation: Workplace Conditions of School Success." In *American Educational Research Journal,* Fall, (12) 3: 325–40.

Lustig, K. 1996. *Portfolio Assessment: A Handbook for Middle Level Teachers.* Columbus, OH: National Middle School Association.

Mabry, L. 1999. *Portfolios Plus: A Critical Guide to Alternative Assessment.* Thousand Oaks, CA: Corwin Press.

Nathan, L. 1995. *Portfolio Assessment and Teacher Practice.* Unpublished doctoral thesis. Harvard Graduate School of Education, Cambridge, MA.

Newmann, F., and Wehlege, G. 1995. *Successful School Restructuring: A Report to the Public and Educators.* Madison, WI: Center on Organization and Restructuring of Schools.

Nguyen, Thanh. *Differential Effects of Multiple Intelligences Curriculum on Student Performance.* Unpublished doctoral thesis. Harvard Graduate School of Education, Cambridge, MA.

Popham, W. James. 1995. *Classroom Assessment: What Teachers Need to Know.* Boston: Allyn and Bacon.

Saphier, J. D., and King, M. 1985 "Good Seeds Grow in Strong Cultures." In *Educational Leadership.* March.

Seidel, S., et al. 1997. *Portfolio Practices: Thinking Through the Assessment of Children's Work.* Washington, D.C.: National Education Association.

Silver, H., et al. 2000. *So Each May Learn: Integrating Learning Styles and Multiple Intelligences.* Alexandria, VA: Association for Supervision and Curriculum Development.

Spurovitz, J. 1994. *The Impact of Portfolio Assessment on Teacher Activities and Student Achievement in Rochester, NY.* Unpublished doctoral thesis. Harvard Graduate School of Education, Cambridge, MA.

Stefanakis, E. H. 1991. "Early Childhood Education: The Effects of Language on Learning." In Ambert, N. (Ed.) *Bilingual Education and English as a Second Language: A Research Handbook, 1988–1990.* New York: Garland.

———. 1993. A Review of the Literature on the Assessment of Young Linguistic Minorities. Unpublished qualifying paper, Harvard Graduate School of Education.

———. 1994. *Preschool Screening: Portfolio Approach for Linguistic Minority Children.* Training Handbook. National Head Start Research. Translating Research into Practice.

————. 1997. "Portfolios: A Way to Sit Beside the Learner." In Veenema, S., S. Seidel, (Eds.). *The Project Zero Classroom.* Cambridge, MA: Harvard Educational Publishing Group.

————. 1998a. *What Is It Like for Students to Use Their Minds Well in an Urban High School?* Documentation of Projects and Portfolios at Fenway Middle College High School. Center for Collaborative Education and the Annenberg Institute.

————. 1998b. *Whose Judgment Counts? Assessing Bilingual Children (K–3).* Portsmouth, NH: Heinemann.

————. 1999. *Teachers' Judgments Do Count: Assessing Bilingual Students.* In Beykont, Z. (Ed.). *Lifting Every Voice: Pedagogy and Politics of Bilingualism,* 139–160. Cambridge, MA: Harvard Education Publishing Group.

————. (in press). *A Portfolio Resource Guide for K–12 Classroom Educators.* (Greek and English). Athens, Greece: Athens College Press.

Stefanakis, E., H. 1997. "The Power in Portfolios: A Way to Sit Beside the Learner." In B. Torff (Ed.) *Multiple Intelligences & Assessment.* Illinois: IRI Skylight.

Tierney, R. et al. 1991. *Portfolio Assessment in the Reading-Writing Classroom.* Norwood, MA: Christopher Gordon Publishers.

Torff, B, ed. 1997. *Multiple Intelligences and Assessment: A Collection of Articles.* Arlington Heights, IL: IRI Skylight.

Underwood, T. 1999. *The Portfolio Project: A Study of Assessment, Instruction and Middle School Reform.* Urbana, IL: National Council of Teachers of English.

Valencia, S., et al. 1994. *Authentic Reading Assessment: Practices and Possibilities.* Newark, DE: International Reading Association.

Multiple Intelligences Web Sites

tqjunior.advanced.org/4376/links.html
literacynet.org/diversity/homenew.html
pzweb.harvard.edu

Index

About the CD-ROM

The CD-ROM for *Multiple Intelligences and Portfolios* contains complete student portfolios and teacher assessment tools.

All of these applications can be accessed directly off the CD-ROM.

Have a question about any of our electronic products? Call or email our tech support hotline: (800) 793-2154 or techsupport@heinemann.com

DATE DUE

DEC 1 2 02		
DEC 2 3		
OCT 0 1 '06		